# UNSEEN
# WEALTH

# UNSEEN WEALTH

## Report of the Brookings Task Force on Intangibles

Margaret M. Blair
and
Steven M. H. Wallman
Task force cochairs

BROOKINGS INSTITUTION PRESS
Washington, D.C.

*Library of Congress Cataloging-in-Publication data*
Blair, Margaret M., 1950–
  Unseen wealth : report of the Brookings Task Force on Intangibles /
Margaret M. Blair and Steven M. H. Wallman.
      p.    cm.
  Includes bibliographical references and index.
  ISBN 0-8157-0113-6
  1. Intangible property—United States—Accounting.
  2. Corporations—Valuation—United States. 3. Research,
Industrial—Economic aspects—United States. 4. Corporation
reports—United States. 5. Gross domestic product—United States.
  I. Wallman, Steven M. H. II. Brookings Task Force on Intangibles.
III. Title.
  HF5681.I55 B55 2001                          2001000218
  658.15—dc21                                  CIP


                    9 8 7 6 5 4 3 2 1

The paper used in this publication meets minimum requirements of the
American National Standard for Information Sciences—-Permanence of Paper for
Printed Library Materials: ANSI Z39.48-1992.

Typeset in Sabon and ITC Officina Sans

Composition by Circle Graphics
Columbia, Maryland

Printed by R. R. Donnelley and Sons
Harrisonburg, Virginia

# Foreword

The dawn of the new century in the United States brought with it a high level of optimism about the general state of the economy. In March 2000 the economic expansion that had started in 1992 became the longest in U.S. history. Although the pace was slowing down by the end of the year, forecasters continued to expect positive growth in output in 2001. Stock prices, although volatile, especially in the high-tech sectors, were still high by historic standards. And in the media and among policymakers there was much excitement about the idea that fundamental changes were transforming the basis for growth in productivity, and thereby increasing the level of economic growth that might be sustainable over the long run.

Regardless of the validity of claims of a "New Economy" and its capacity for continued growth, one change in the way the economy operates seems almost indisputable: economic growth is no longer being driven primarily by investments in physical assets, but instead by investments in intellectual, organizational, institutional, and reputational assets. The factors that have become most important to business success and economic growth in developed economies in the twenty-first century are "intangible," or "nonphysical." By their very nature, intangibles are harder to measure, harder to quantify, and often more difficult to manage, evaluate, and account for than tangible assets. For the most part, they do not appear on the balance sheets of corporations, nor are they recorded in the national accounts as part of national wealth.

This report argues that the large and growing discrepancy between the importance of intangible assets to economic growth and the ability to identify, measure, and account for those assets is a serious potential problem for business managers, for investors, and for government. The product of two years of discussion and research by a special task force on intangibles convened by the Brookings Institution, it examines the dimensions of the problem and recommends actions that government and business can and should responsibly take at this time to begin to improve the quality and quantity of available information about intangible investments at the firm level, at the level of specific industries, and at the level of the aggregate economy. In doing so, it focuses mainly on information problems, which the task force views as a necessary first step toward addressing the optimal allocation of resources in a rapidly changing economy.

For financial support of the Brookings Project on Understanding Intangible Sources of Value, of which the task force's report is a part, the authors are grateful to Kenichi Ikeda as well as the following organizations: the American Society for Training and Development; Arthur Andersen; Dickstein, Shapiro, Morin and Oshinsky; Dow Chemical Co.; Ernst and Young; IBM Corp.; Pfizer Corp.; PricewaterhouseCoopers; the SEC and Financial Reporting Institute at University of Southern California; Skandia AFS; the Alfred P. Sloan Foundation; Steelcase Inc.; Thermo-Electron Corp.; and Valuation Research Corp. In addition, PricewaterhouseCoopers provided valuable staff support.

The authors also thank Amy Barrett, Charlene Mui, Christopher Nekarda, Patricia Powers, Michael Prosser, and Hannah Zweibel for research and staff assistance; Catherine Theohary for research verification; and Kimberley Bliss and Caleb Patten for assistance in setting up the project's website. At the Brookings Institution Press, Tanjam Jacobson ably edited the manuscript, Inge Lockwood proofread the pages, and Sherry Smith provided the index.

The findings and recommendations presented here have been endorsed generally by the business leaders, consultants, accounting professionals, economists, intellectual property lawyers, policy analysts, and others who participated on the task force (see appendix for a full list). While they do not all necessarily agree with every detail, they all do generally agree with the broad principles, objectives, and policy responses laid out. The views expressed in the report should not, however, be ascribed to the trustees, officers, or staff members of the Brookings Institution or the home institutions of the named task force members, nor to any individual or organization listed above who generously supported the work of the task force.

MICHAEL H. ARMACOST
*President, Brookings Institution*

*Washington, D.C.*
*March 2001*

# Contents

# Introduction

As the United States and other developed economies move into the twenty-first century, the factors that have become most important to economic growth and societal wealth are "intangible," or "nonphysical": intellectual capital, research and development (R&D), brand names, human capital are examples. In this "New Economy," economic growth is no longer being driven primarily by investments in physical assets, such as factories, machines, office buildings, farm land, and mineral resources, but instead by investments in intellectual, organizational, institutional, and reputational assets. To cite an extreme example, as of the end of September 2000 Microsoft Corp. had only $1.9 billion in property and equipment. But its market capitalization was about $328 billion.[1]

Similarly, Merck and Co., Inc., and Pfizer, Inc., have prospered not because they have built new factories for manufacturing and packaging pills, but because they have been technological leaders, spending substantial amounts on research and development to develop new pharmaceuticals.[2] Walmart did not become the largest retailing company in the country just because it built more and bigger stores, but because it developed a unique and highly efficient inventory control and distribution system, and then used its purchasing clout to compel its suppliers to make efficiency-enhancing changes in their operations.[3] And the wealth of Silicon Valley is not, for the most part, bricks and mortar wealth. Rather, it is based on the digitization of ideas. Even "old economy" manufacturing companies have come to understand that brand and image may be as, or more, important to their ability to make profits as is the number of new machines they buy for their factories.[4]

By their nature, intangibles are harder to measure, to quantify, to manage—harder even to define—than tangibles. For the most part, they do not appear on the balance sheets of corporations, nor are they recorded in the national accounts as part of the national wealth. When they are acquired or developed, they are treated more like consumption than as additions to net worth. Indeed, there is no common language for talking about intangible sources of value, and what language there is tends to be ad hoc and descriptive rather than quantitative and concrete, making comparisons from one institutional situation to the next impossible.

The individuals who participated in the discussions and research underlying this report believe that the large and growing discrepancy between the importance of intangible assets to economic growth and the ability to clearly identify, measure, and account for those assets is a serious potential problem for business managers, investors, and government. In this report, we assess the problem and make policy recommendations for business and government that we believe would improve the quality and reliability of information about the intangible sources of value in the economy. We believe that, over time, better information will lead to better resource allocation decisions, as well as greater stability and perceived fairness in capital markets.

We define intangibles as nonphysical factors that contribute to or are used in producing goods or providing services, or that are expected to generate future productive benefits for the individuals or firms that control the use of those factors. Evidence that intangibles are gaining in economic importance includes the growth of services as a share of total economic activity; the rapid climb in the value of financial assets over the past decade and a half, despite relatively low growth in physical assets (such as property, plant, and equipment); and a swelling body of anecdotal evidence from firms about what is important to them and their need for new measurement and management information tools.

For a variety of reasons, existing accounting rules do not provide good information about investments in intangibles made by firms. Where markets have been created for certain kinds of intangible assets (patent licenses or film rights, for example), values may be determined for these assets. And if there is a transaction in which such assets are exchanged, they may even get recorded on the books of the individual companies involved. Some firms have also developed internal metrics for measuring and monitoring nonfinancial performance. But the state of the art in the development of alternative business models and information systems is still rudimentary, ad hoc, and situation specific.

The lack of good information about intangibles leads to problems in measuring important macroeconomic variables that are used to guide public policy. It also makes resource allocation and investment decisions within firms and across firms in a given industry much more difficult. It leads to opaqueness, volatility, and perceptions of unfairness in capital markets, and it makes designing a fair tax system more difficult.

Meanwhile, efforts to develop better business reporting models and better information capture systems are hampered by a public goods problem: better information would benefit everyone, but no individual firm has an incentive to incur the large costs of developing such an information system on its own. Efforts have also been slowed by the historic conservatism of the accounting and regulatory communities and concerns about competitiveness and liability among the business community. For a variety of reasons noted below, even the investment community has not pushed hard to require firms to report more information. But the most important impediments to development of better information on intangibles are the cognitive barriers—the lack of business models that accurately and effectively describe productive activities in the New Economy and the lack of a common vocabulary with clear, consistent, and robust definitions of the factors that go into such productive activity.

In chapter 1 we lay out evidence that intangibles have become a primary source of value in the business community and we explain the problems of current accounting and financial reporting systems and their weaknesses in providing relevant information about intangibles. We also detail some of the problems that result from the lack of good information. In chapter 2 we examine some of the actual and potential barriers to developing and providing better information about investment in intangibles. In chapter 3 we briefly examine the historic role of government in the creation of intangibles. And in chapters 4 through 8 we present our findings and recommendations. We argue that, while business bears the primary responsibility for developing better metrics for measuring business and economic performance, at least within individual firms, government actions can contribute in at least three areas to facilitate, or reduce barriers to, private sector efforts to overcome these problems:

*Data building.* First, we recommend government funding and support for a large public-private project to assemble new data sources needed by the private sector to construct reliable, sensible business models and metrics that better reflect the dynamics of wealth creation in the twenty-first century. These data would also provide important inputs for the development of new macroeconomic performance measures and the revision of old measures. This project might be carried out by some combination of the Bureau of Economic Analysis at the Department of Commerce, the Center for Economic Studies at the Census Bureau, the Bureau of Labor Statistics at the Department of Labor, and the National Science Foundation. The agencies that took on this project would have to work in collaboration with firms in the private sector.

*Corporate disclosure.* Second, we call for the Securities and Exchange Commission (SEC) and the Financial Accounting Standards Board (FASB), which together set financial reporting rules for public companies, to monitor this project, with an eye toward identifying reliable performance indicators that should be included in the disclosures required of publicly traded companies. A few companies have made cautious and tentative attempts at increasing the amount of information they provide to investors. And both the FASB and the SEC have formed committees to consider what expanded disclosure should be encouraged or required. But much more needs to be done.

More immediately, we recommend that these bodies move now to require greater breakout of cost information by type of expenditure at the business segment level, where feasible, as well as expanded discussion of factors that drive value creation by management in public disclosure documents. We also propose that the SEC expand the safe harbor protections for firms that voluntarily disclose more information about their intangibles and value drivers.

*Intellectual property.* Third, we recommend a series of changes and adjustments in intellectual property rights laws to increase the certainty of legal protection for patents, trademarks, and trade secrets.

We believe that action in these three areas could form the foundation for greatly improved public and private information about the factors that are most important to economic success in the years ahead.

# CHAPTER ONE

# The Problem

*"Given that no company can establish a monopoly on brains,
how do you keep the people that make it work? There are no tangible
assets to divest. There is intellectual property and that's about it—
and a building."*

Attorney Lloyd Cutler,
commenting on the proposed breakup of Microsoft
(*Washington Post*, April 29, 2000, p. A1).

The U.S. economy, like the economies of most industrial countries, is increasingly one in which the "products" that firms provide are not simply physical goods but are services or experiences. Even the physical goods we buy are greatly enhanced in their value to us by the technology embedded in them or by the brand image they carry. Indeed, market services and intangible goods now account for more than two-thirds of gross domestic product (GDP) in the United States.[5]

A critical difference between an economy that is based on the production, trade, and consumption of physical goods and an economy that involves extensive trade in services, experiences, technology, and ideas is that the former can be readily measured. It is extremely difficult to measure the volume of trade in the latter in any units other than the price paid for them. Likewise, it is difficult to quantify the investment and expenditure of resources required to produce intangible goods or to assess whether expenditures on

Market services and intangible goods account for more than two-thirds of U.S. GDP. Some day-to-day examples:

**Services**
financial or legal advice
insurance
education
nursing
child care
physical therapy
hotel stays
catering
Internet connections
telephone and cable
    connections
air travel

**Embedded technology in**
extra memory or
    computing power
anti-lock car brakes
the latest allergy
    medications
reduced cholesterol
    mayonnaise
vitamin-enriched cereals
high-performance fibers
    in athletic wear

**Experiences**
concerts
movies
sports events
restaurant meals, from
    elegant cuisine to
    "fast" food
sky diving
bungee jumping
cruises

**Brand images**
Nike footwear
Coca-Cola
Rolex watches
Starbucks coffee
Tommy Hilfiger denim
    pants
Ralph Lauren bed
    linens

the inputs into the production of intangibles are well spent. How does one measure the capacity of an economy to exchange services, experiences, technology, and ideas?[6] How does one measure national wealth in this kind of an economy? How does one know whether the economy is growing or shrinking, whether productivity is increasing and how fast, whether one company is performing better than another, or whether our citizens are better off this year than they were last year? Perhaps most important, how do we know whether we are, individually or as a nation, making investments that will increase productivity and economic wealth in the years ahead?

This report is about the vast uncertainty around such questions and its implications both for public policy and for the allocation of investment resources by the private sector. In particular, it focuses on the problem of providing accurate and useful information about the intangible inputs into such an economy—the ideas, special skills, organizational structures and capabilities, brand identities, mailing lists and data bases, and the networks of social, professional, and business relationships that make it possible for hundreds of millions of people to exchange services, experiences, technology, and ideas.[7]

## The Importance of Intangibles

*Intangibles* is a difficult term to define. One reason for the lack of consensus about a definition is that the elements of what could or should be regarded as intangibles depend on whether one is talking about accounting concepts or measures of national income and wealth or how to develop and manage the nonphysical inputs into a business. For purposes of this analysis, the task force adopted the following broad definition: intangibles are nonphysical factors that contribute to, or are used in, the production of goods or the provision of services or that are expected to generate future productive benefits to the individuals or firms that control their use.[8]

*Intangibles are nonphysical factors that contribute to, or are used in, the production of goods or the provision of services or that are expected to generate future productive benefits to the individuals or firms that control their use.*

Historically, intangibles have not been treated as part of national wealth, nor have they generally been accounted for as part of the assets of firms. In 1911 Irving Fisher defined economics as "the science of wealth" and defined wealth as "material objects owned by human beings."[9] These definitions have formed the basis of the measurement conventions used in the national accounts. Similarly, business accounting was developed to keep track of transactions that enhance or diminish the assets of firms. Here again, the convention has been that only physical items or intangibles purchased in arms-length transactions (such as patents) should count as assets, whereas other inputs have to be counted as services and treated as transitory.

Yet intangibles are important in the production, marketing, and distribution of physical goods as well as the delivery of services. Intangibles are not the same as services, but they are linked, and the delivery of highly skilled services and professional services involves substantial inputs of intangibles. How important have intangibles become? This report grew out of the concern that data on the role of intangibles in the economy is seriously inadequate. But even the indirect evidence gives strong reason to believe that the economic importance of intangibles is growing rapidly.

### Role of Services in the Economy

Services have increased steadily as a share of measured total output in the United States, from 22 percent of GDP in 1950 to about 39 percent in 1999.[10] Intangibles such as skills and professional knowledge, organizational capabilities, reputational capital, mailing lists and other collections of data, are important factors in the provision of many services.

### Value of Financial Claims

*Intangibles are not the same as services but the two are linked, and the delivery of highly skilled services and complex professional services involves substantial inputs of intangibles. The share of services in measured total output has been increasing steadily in the U.S. economy, from 22 percent of GDP in 1950 to about 39 percent in 1999.*

Although investments in intangibles such as R&D, brand name development, and software systems are generally not recorded as part of the book value of corporations (unless they were purchased externally), outside investors recognize their worth and tend to place high value on firms with high levels of these sorts of investments. In the past twenty years, there has been a rapid increase in the total value of financial claims and securities issued by the corporate sector (debt plus equity), despite low growth in tangibles; only a small part of this increase can be accounted for by purchases of physical capital or even by inflation in the value of existing physical capital. Economist Robert Hall has analyzed the rather large discrepancy that has developed in the past decade between the value assigned to firms by the financial markets and the value recorded on their books. He concludes that this empirical discrepancy can only be reconciled with financial theories about how stocks are valued if "corporations own substantial amounts of intangible capital not recorded in the sector's books or anywhere in government statistics." He has since named this unrecorded intangible capital "e-capital." [11]

Hall's analysis is based on aggregate economic data for all nonfarm, nonfinancial corporations, but the same conclusion seems almost inescapable if one looks at the balance sheets of even a few individual firms. As of early August 2000, for example, the market value of Walt Disney Co. stock totaled around $83 billion, and the firm also had about $34 billion in outstanding liabilities, for a total market capitalization of $117 billion. But on the books the firm had only $43.7 billion in assets. This total included some $11.3 billion worth of recognized intangible assets. Apparently the financial markets thought that Disney had closer to $85 billion worth of intangibles— almost eight times the recognized book value of such assets. Similarly, Sprint Corp. had a total market capitalization of $60.2 billion in early August 2000, compared with $39 billion in book assets, which included $9.6 billion in recognized intangibles. Here again, the financial markets apparently thought that Sprint had nearly $31 billion worth of intangibles, more than three times what its balance sheet showed. The remarkable bull market in stocks— and especially the huge run up in technology and Internet stock prices—over the past decade cooled somewhat in the last few months of 2000, but not nearly enough to change the analysis. In fact, equity prices would have to fall by two-thirds or more, across the board, for the significant discrepancy between market value and book value to disappear. [12]

Cross-sectional evidence on firms also suggests that some significant part of the discrepancy between market value and book value is due to investments in intangibles.[13] The discrepancy is greatest in firms that are known to have been investing most heavily in certain kinds of intangible complements to computers. Erik Brynjolfsson and Shinkyu Yang, for example, find a strong correlation between the total value of computers in a corporation and the implicit value assigned to the intangibles in that corporation by the stock market. "It is not that the market values a dollar of computers at $10," Robert Hall observes about this finding. "Rather, the firm that has a dollar of computers typically has another $9 of related intangibles."[14] Likewise, Timothy Bresnahan, Brynjolfsson, and Lorin Hitt find that firms that invest heavily in computer technology get the greatest boost in productivity if they invest simultaneously in human capital—upgrading the skills of their work force—and in organizational capital, specifically, by restructuring work to devolve decisionmaking authority downward and outward within the firm to rank and file employees.[15]

Other studies have found that firms in key growth industries (the high-tech, life sciences, and business services sectors) tend to have high ratios of R&D spending to sales, and, in turn, firms with high levels of spending on R&D tend to have high ratios of market value to book value.[16] Studies also show that the firms that make the greatest investments in the education and training of their work force have above average productivity and

*A significant part of the current discrepancy between market value and book value of firms appears due to investments in intangibles. Equity prices would have to fall by two-thirds or more, across the board, for this discrepancy to disappear.*

financial performance.[17] Taken together, these findings suggest that stock prices, although they are an extremely noisy signal, probably have at least some validity as an indicator of the growing role of intangibles in the economy.

### Anecdotal Evidence from Firms

Another indication that intangibles are among corporations' most important investments is the accumulating anecdotal evidence from firms themselves. The Conference Board, for example, has produced two major studies that reveal substantial corporate interest in developing new and better measures of performance that go beyond financial measures alone. The most recent study reports that companies are developing indicators to measure "activities and processes . . . such as the development of intellectual capital, and improving customer satisfaction and retention as well as workplace practices. . . . In many cases, these 'intangibles' provide the best indicator of a company's potential for growth." It also cites evidence that institutional investors are interested in knowing more about these intangible investments.[18] Interest in these issues has exploded in the past few years and months, and the major accounting and consulting firms are pouring resources into projects to help their clients develop better business models and better measures of performance.[19]

*Corporate executives have come to see human capital investment as a source of competitive advantage.*

Human capital investments have come to be seen by many corporate executives as a source of competitive advantage. This intuition is confirmed by research over the past ten to fifteen years demonstrating that investments in bundles of innovative work practices (sometimes called high-performance work systems) in areas such as training, job design, selection, staffing, employee involvement, labor-management cooperation, and incentive compensation positively impact firm performance.[20] The reputation of the chief executive officer (CEO) has also been shown to be important to business success.[21] In their advertising, companies are increasingly emphasizing their technical leadership, the speed and quality of their service, and the sophistication, commitment, and skills of their employees. Yet factual information about investments in intangible resources is conspicuously lacking from most companies' annual reports and 10-K filings.[22]

## Measurement Difficulties

One major reason why good, hard data on the importance of intangible assets in the economy are not available is that intangibles are inherently difficult to measure, quantify, and account for. Because one cannot see, or touch, or weigh intangibles, one cannot measure them directly but must instead rely on proxies, or indirect measures, to say something about their impact on some other variable that can be measured.

*Because one cannot see, or touch, or weigh intangibles, one cannot measure them directly but must instead rely on proxies, or indirect measures, to say something about their impact on some other variable that can be measured.*

Just as one cannot answer the question "How satisfied are the company's customers?" in the same one-dimensional way as one can answer "How many hamburgers did the company sell?" one cannot measure how much customer loyalty a firm's advertising campaign created in the same way as one can measure how much office space the firm added with its new building. To be sure, assigning value to many *tangible* assets may require considerable subjective judgment, but while valuing tangibles can be difficult, valuing *intangibles* is generally a much more complex proposition.

### Accounting Rules

Accounting rules are designed to record what happens in specific transactions and thereby track the flows of assets into and out of a corporation. Under the accounting principles used in the United States and in most developed countries, for resources to be considered assets they must be well defined and distinct from other assets, the firm must have effective control over them, it must be possible to predict the future economic benefits from them, and it must be possible to determine whether their economic value has been impaired (for example, through depreciation or depletion) and to what extent.[23] These criteria mean that the term *assets* is generally interpreted to mean property, plant, and equipment; financial assets; and purchased identifiable intangible assets, such as patents, trademarks, and mailing lists.

To be sure, accountants have long understood the need to recognize some assets that do not fit neatly into any of these categories. "Purchased goodwill" is one of the few additional categories recognized in the United States, however.[24] When company A acquires company B, for example, A adds B's net assets (assets minus liabilities) to the net assets on its own balance sheet. If B has $500 million worth of property, plant, and equipment, financial, and other identifiable assets and zero liabilities on its books, those assets will be added to the books of A. But suppose that A has paid $750 million for B. How does it account for the additional $250 million that are not reflected in B's book value? If possible, A would first "write-up," or assign a higher value—based on appraisals—to, the acquired hard assets. Then it would assign a value to any specific intangibles that could be identified and valued. Finally, A would add the remaining amount (say $200 million) to its books as goodwill. Goodwill, rather than referring to specific assets, is just a catch-all residual category, a label given to the going concern value of assets in the target company over and above those that can be kicked, or counted, or weighed, or valued with some precision.

Other than purchased goodwill, accounting rules generally require that internal expenditures on such intangible assets as R&D, training, advertising, and promotion be "expensed," that is, treated as expenses in the period in which they are incurred and charged against current earnings. This implies that the inputs paid for by those expenses are used up in production in the period in which the expenses are incurred, and that such expenditures do not create any asset that will provide an input into future production.

Within the accounting profession, there has been growing debate over whether this treatment is appropriate, especially for R&D. A number of scholars have argued that expenditures on R&D should be treated as investments, just like expenditures on new plant or equipment. When a company spends money on a new warehouse, for example, the expenditures are not treated as expenses in the current period but are recorded as a reduction in cash assets and an addition to the plant and equipment assets of the firm. In each subsequent period, the company records a charge

*The debate over the accounting treatment of R&D turns on whether it ought to be understood as a current cost of doing business, and therefore expensed, or it should be capitalized, on the grounds that these expenditures are adding an asset to the firm.*

against current earnings to reflect the fact that some of the value of the asset has been used up or worn out. This accounting treatment is called "capitalizing" the expenditure, and the subsequent periodic charges against earnings are called "depreciation." Thus the debate over the accounting treatment of R&D is a question about whether R&D ought to be understood as a current cost of doing business, and therefore expensed, or it should be capitalized, on the theory that the expenditures are adding an asset to the firm.[25]

Indeed, there is disagreement among prominent accounting standards bodies worldwide about how to record R&D expenditures. The International Accounting Standards Committee (IASC) requires that research be expensed, but development costs that meet certain criteria must be capitalized. In the United Kingdom, the Accounting Standards Board (ASB) requires expensing of research but permits development to be capitalized. And in Japan, the accounting profession permits capitalization of research, development, and a range of other internally generated intangibles. In the United States, however, the Financial Accounting Standards Board requires full expensing of R&D, except for the final development stages of potential software products.[26]

If measuring, quantifying, and accounting for R&D assets is difficult, human capital poses even greater challenges. To be sure, the accounting treatment is well defined and not particularly controversial: wage and nonwage labor costs are expensed in the same accounting period as the labor services are performed, unless the costs are associated with the building of fixed assets or the manufacture of products that are added to asset inventories. In these cases, labor costs are expensed as the assets produced by the labor services are sold or depreciated.

To the extent that such costs are associated with ongoing operations, this makes sense. The costs of labor services are

reported either in the same period as the services are provided or in the period in which the products generated by
the services are sold or used up. But to the extent that some
of the expenditures on labor (such as for training, team
building, and reorganization) generate benefits in future
periods, this accounting treatment produces a distortion.
Because such expenditures never show up on the company's
balance sheets as an asset, they are not managed in the same
way as other assets, and the firm can only guess at the rate
of return it gets on them. When a firm is acquired and the
acquiring firm adds goodwill to its books, that goodwill
may reflect the value of a skilled work force in the acquired
company. Yet this is not transparent. Moreover, in future
periods the acquiring firm must take a charge against its
earnings for depreciation of the goodwill, even if it is simultaneously recording the expenses associated with investments in maintaining the asset through training or updating
the know-how, competences, and skills of the workers.

A final reason why the traditional accounting model has not been very helpful in providing information about intangible assets to business managers is that accounting rules are designed to record and track discrete and sequential transactions and to show their cumulative effect. The value created by investments in intangibles is rarely tied to

*The value created by investments in intangibles is rarely tied to discrete transactions. Rather, it is often highly contextual and dependent on complementary investments in other intangibles.*

discrete transactions, however. Rather, it is often highly
contextual and dependent on complementary investments
in other intangibles. The value of a brand, for example, may
depend on patent rights to some underlying technology as

well as expenditures on advertising or other reputation-enhancing activities. Furthermore, the process of creating valuable intangible assets is not always linear or direct. A "failure" in an R&D program might lead to insights that interact with the findings from another program and end up creating value in unexpected ways.[27] And value can be destroyed in similarly unexpected and indirect ways.[28]

### Other Measures

If accounting models do not generally produce good measures of intangibles, are there other measures that do? So far the answer appears to be maybe, for some assets, in some situations, and for some purposes.

For example, stock and bond prices provide a measure of the value that financial markets place on the financial claims (debt plus equity) of individual corporations. This value can be viewed as a claim on the aggregate value of the physical and financial assets of those corporations plus the value of the intangible assets, or the going concern value, in those corporations. Thus, as indicated above, one can look at the difference between the market value of the financial claims against a corporation and the value of its tangible assets and come up with a measure of the financial market's estimate of the value of that firm's intangible assets.

*Securities backed by financial assets, such as receivables, have been issued for many years, but only in the past five or six years have firms and financial institutions put together a significant number of ABS deals backed by intellectual property.*

A few companies and creative financial institutions have also been attempting to "securitize" the income streams from bundles of intangible assets, especially intellectual property, by using financial instruments such as asset-backed securities (ABSs). These are debt securities for which the issuing companies have pledged the cash flow (often enhanced by third-party guarantees) from some collection of assets or some subset of the firm's business. ABSs backed by financial assets, such as receivables, have been issued for many years, but only in the past five or six years have firms and financial institutions put together a significant number of deals based on intellectual property.[29] Implicit in the fact that the lending institutions are willing to buy the securities backed by these assets is the notion that it is possible to estimate the value of the pledged intangible assets.[30]

These measures of securitized intangibles may be a useful indicator of how important intangibles have become in individual firms. And the aggregate difference between the value of financial claims and the value of tangible assets says something about their importance in the economy as a whole. But such measures have serious drawbacks for other purposes. The market prices of financial assets are notoriously volatile and noisy indicators of underlying value. They also provide only an aggregated measure and give no hint about the nature of the specific assets, resources, or other factors that produce that value, let alone the factors that might enhance or diminish that value. Hence financial asset prices, by themselves, are currently of limited use to managers for day-to-day decisions about investing in or using intangibles and preserving or enhancing their value.

Although the implicit information in ABS issues is, perhaps, useful at the level of individual firms, intellectual property ABSs have so far only been issued in private placements to financial institutions, and there is no public market in these instruments. Moreover, the details of such transactions are usually confidential. Thus, although such transactions suggest that certain intangible assets can be valued, the information on value that they yield is not shared as well as it might be with other investors or the market as a whole.[31]

As noted in the previous chapter, however, there is empirical evidence that expenditures on certain kinds of intangibles development, especially R&D, are generally reflected in higher stock prices.[32] This suggests that participants in financial markets are somehow gathering and interpreting information about intangibles, even if that information is not formally reported by companies in their public documents or otherwise widely shared with investors.

In attempting to get behind the aggregate story told by stock prices, a number of companies, organizations, and individuals have developed measures for internal use. These have been used to help measure and monitor nonfinancial performance and to show the linkages among the intangible factors that contribute to that performance, as well as the link between nonfinancial and financial performance.[33] Some of these measures have gained a certain prominence and have apparently proved to be useful management tools in individual companies. None, however, is being used consistently by a large enough group of firms to provide useful cross-sectional or time-series data, or even reasonable benchmarks that one company could use to compare its performance with that of another. So far, at least, the information generated by these efforts is still ad hoc and situation specific. As the Strategic Organizational Issues subgroup of the task force concluded, "companies have no coherent, consistent or regular approaches to representing, managing, and valuing their intangibles. . . . Investment decisions in the area of intangibles seem more a matter of faith than fact."[34]

**Consequences of Poor Measurement** What harm, if any, comes from the fact that there is currently no way to quantify or, in many cases, even articulate and describe in clear comparable terms the factors that lead to better business performance? It is known, in general, that education and training are important in producing a skilled work force; that innovation is important; that market share is valuable; and that brands, reputation, and image are important factors in gaining market share. Does it matter that it seems hard to be more specific? It is the job, the creative act, if you will, of management to make resource allocation decisions and to engage employees, business partners, and other participants in value-creating activities. Does it matter that this creative process is still fundamentally quite mysterious?

The task force believes that not being able to identify and measure the intangible inputs into wealth creation creates substantial costs for society. Although many of these costs are unavoidable, this project has been motivated by the belief that one could know more than is known, and that because of the high costs of not knowing, it is worth expending resources to learn. Below, we briefly review some of the costs of not knowing.

### National Accounts

In the United States, large amounts of data on the performance of the economy are collected and developed each year by the federal government (and the governments of other countries). Much of the data for the national accounts are developed by aggregating up from individual or firm-level data or projecting from survey data to produce measures such as GDP, corporate profits, personal savings, aggregate capital stock, productivity, and inflation. The national accounts are used in setting a variety of policies. In 1999 and 2000, for example, the Federal Reserve Board was concerned about the rapid growth rate of measured GDP, the low unemployment rate, and the high capital utilization rate, fearing that an overheated economy might lead to increased inflation. So the Fed increased interest rates in hopes of slowing down economic activity. Was this the right response, or was the U.S. economy now capable of higher sustained levels of economic growth without inflation?

In the early 1990s, many policymakers were concerned about projected deficits in the federal budget and took actions (in the form of tax increases and spending cuts) to reduce those deficits. But the U.S. economy performed far better in the 1990s than anyone might have hoped six or eight years earlier, and by 2000 the federal budget was producing substantial surpluses. Why were the forecasts so far off the mark? And today policymakers are concerned about the ability of the economy to provide for millions of retiring baby boomers in the near future. What kinds of investments are needed today to boost productivity ten, twenty, or thirty years down the road? These and other serious questions of public policy cry out for a better understanding of the role of intangible assets in the economy.[35]

There is good reason to believe that the failure to account adequately for investments in intangibles results in the understatement of GDP, of corporate profits, and of personal savings because accounting systems that treat investments in intangibles as expenses thereby overstate the costs of producing current output. Leonard Nakamura has argued, for example, that if corporate expenditures on R&D had been capitalized instead of expensed, measured corporate profits would have been higher in recent years, and stock prices in 1999 relative to these adjusted profits would not have been seriously out of line with historic experience, nor seen as a matter of policy concern.[36] Measured GDP would also have been higher if R&D had been capitalized. To the extent that expenditures on other kinds of intangibles (such as marketing, human resource development, and software development) were increasing as a share of GDP in the 1990s, the same argument would apply; measured profits and output would have been even higher, and price-earnings ratios would seem more reasonable by historic standards.

*The failure to understand the role of intangible assets in the aggregate economy will lead repeatedly to misdiagnoses of economic problems and inappropriate policy responses.*

More generally, it seems likely that the failure to understand the role of intangible assets in the aggregate economy will lead repeatedly to misdiagnoses of economic problems and inappropriate policy responses.

### Capital Markets

It is widely accepted that stock prices tend to incorporate some information about intangibles. However, a variety of disclosure problems stem from the lack of transparency of the information and the process by which investors learn about and act on this information. These problems likely increase the cost of capital and reduce the perceived fairness of the capital markets to individual investors.[37]

The requirements for disclosure of key corporate financial information in the United States are among the most extensive and stringent in the world. Corporations are required to file detailed financial information with the

Securities and Exchange Commission when they first register their securities for public trading, and they must provide a full and detailed update annually, condensed interim reports every quarter, and immediate updates in the case of extraordinary events. These extensive disclosure requirements are a central part of a corporate governance and financial system that, more than any other in the world, has encouraged small investors to invest in corporate equities. The result has been a powerful engine for turning personal savings into investments, investments into technical advances, and technical advances into economic growth. But the effectiveness of disclosure requirements at ensuring good corporate governance and performance is being eroded, because as intangibles become more important relative to tangible assets, this required disclosure reveals less about the real assets and sources of value inside a firm.

Baruch Lev argues, for example, that commonly used performance measures, such as return on equity or return on total assets, become much less useful in intangibles-intensive firms, because "major investments are missing from the denominator."[38] Likewise, the human capital assets of firms—their reserve of skills, competencies, and knowhow and the resources being expended to renew and expand them—are beyond the spectrum of information that is typically available to investors. The lack of clear, quantifiable, and comparable information about intangibles-intensive companies tends to encourage selective disclosure of inside information to key investors, making it easier for people with inside information to gain at the expense of outsiders and small investors.

In fact, by the summer of 2000 the SEC had become so concerned about the tendency of listed firms to make selective disclosures that it approved a new regulation requiring companies to release material market-moving information to all investors simultaneously. Under Regulation FD, if a company purposefully or inadvertently discloses selective information, in a phone call from an analyst, for example, the company must publicly release and publicize this information within twenty-four hours.[39] Critics argue that this will simply discourage companies from releasing any information that is not required, rather than encouraging them to issue more information more widely and more fairly.[40] While selective release of information might make small investors more cautious than they would be otherwise, a reduction in information is likely to make all investors more cautious. However, if the capital markets demand more information, and this is provided universally, as Regulation FD intends, then all investors will benefit as measures and information now provided only selectively become more transparent.

Against this, it might be noted, as of the close of 2000, even after significant decreases in valuations in the technology sector, many "dot-com" and other high-tech companies were commanding high price-earnings ratios. Since many of these companies have virtually no assets except for their intangibles (a concept, a copyright perhaps, and the willingness of a cadre of eager twenty-eight-year-olds to work fourteen hours a day, seven days a week for stock options), it is hard to make the case that intangibles-intensive firms cannot get capital, or even that the cost of capital is too high. But, at least for the time being, investor sentiment has grown more cautious of this sector and

*More comprehensive and more reliable information about intangibles in high-tech companies would reduce information asymmetry and the associated market volatility and restore market confidence.*

support could weaken further. More comprehensive and more reliable information about intangibles in such companies would help reduce the problems of information asymmetry and the associated costs in market volatility for the sector as a whole.[41] Moreover, better information would lead to better decisions about which specific companies and ideas should be funded and which should not. This, in turn, would help to restore overall market confidence.

### Industries

At the level of specific industries, lack of good data on intangibles and their contribution to productivity and performance may lead to a misallocation of resources, both within firms and between firms in the same industry. As economist Joseph Stiglitz notes, "If we are going to know what are high-return activities and we want our resources to be allocated towards high-return activities, we have to have accurate ways of measuring what those returns are."[42]

One of the factors that could lead to a misallocation of resources within an industry is the perfectly reasonable tendency of investors to compare the performance of individual companies against their industry peers. But the validity of this approach depends on whether the industry benchmarks used in such a comparison are good indicators of future performance. Comparisons of asset levels, investment rates, or profit rates without some adjustment for investments in intangibles are likely to be very misleading. Data on expenditures on training, patent citations, number of Ph.D.s on the staff, share of revenues from new products, new product development times, or other indicators of the firms' investments in intangibles could provide more insight into the relative performance of companies—if such data were available.

### Companies

Other significant costs arising from the lack of good knowledge about the role of intangible assets in the economy are those that affect individual companies. Today, good management practice demands greater sophistication about the contribution of intangibles to the strategic performance of a company. Managers need to know which activities to encourage, what kinds of investments to make, and what kinds to avoid to improve overall performance. They also need to be able to communicate a strategic vision to employees throughout the firm, a game plan for how to achieve that vision, and a set of interim goals and measurements that will provide feedback on their progress. Although good management has always involved elements of intuition and gut instinct, managers themselves concede that their poor understanding of the role of intangibles makes it harder for them to judge the performance of individual employees or teams within the firm, as well as the true costs and benefits of a large share of their business activity.

One indication that some firms consider the costs of not knowing substantial is the energy they are devoting to the development of internal nonstandard and nonfinancial measures of performance. Examples of such measures observed by members of the task force include profitable revenue growth, market share, product acquisition costs, market requirements and specifications, time to break even in profits, time from conception to market for new products, competitor responses, schedule slip rates, percent of revenue created by products that have been in the market less than some given amount of time, and number of new products created on each technology platform. Some companies also face external pressure to develop and provide information on what might be called "social performance," such as environmental performance, workplace safety, and wages and working conditions in factories run by subcontractors. In these areas, not knowing may not seem like a problem until something goes seriously wrong and the company is suddenly faced with lawsuits or substantial reputational costs.[43]

### Taxation

Another public policy problem that is exacerbated by the growing importance of intangible assets in the economy is the problem of identifying a fair, useful, and feasible basis for assessing tax liabilities and collecting taxes. This issue has already arisen in a highly public way in the controversy over whether online commercial transactions ("e-commerce") ought to escape sales taxes at the state level. When an individual buys a washing machine in an appliance store, it is relatively easy to identify the jurisdiction in which the transaction took place for sales tax purposes. But when an individual buys an online subscription to an electronic magazine, downloads it at work in Washington, D.C., and reads it at home in Maryland, the rules about which jurisdiction, if any, may tax that transaction and who is supposed to collect the tax and pass it along to the taxing authorities become much less clear.

Leaving aside e-commerce, intangible assets raise a number of tax policy concerns similar to those raised in the context of financial accounting. For example, should the costs of creating an intangible asset be deducted when incurred or depreciated over an expected useful life of the asset? How does one determine the appropriate transfer prices for exchanges of intellectual property rights, licenses, and other intangibles among international subsidiaries of a corporation when there is no comparable public market for these goods? If tangible assets are subject to state and local property taxes, is it appropriate also to levy these taxes on intangible assets? More broadly, how does the tax treatment of intangible assets affect the efficient allocation of resources in the economy?

# CHAPTER TWO

# Barriers to Better Information

The lack of good information about the role of intangibles in the economy is itself the most obvious and important barrier to developing better information. Both economic models of production and accounting models of firm performance are, essentially, input-output-type models. They are designed to measure the inputs into a production process and the outputs from that process. These traditional measures have proved to be quite robust in providing the information necessary to track the performance of sectors of the economy that produce goods—agriculture, mining, manufacturing, and even transportation and utilities.

They are turning out to be much less robust, however, in providing information relevant to the performance of the service- and information-based sectors of the economy—health care, legal services, financial services, personal services, education, entertainment, media, software. In these sectors, "quantitative" measures of both "inputs" and "outputs" may be almost meaningless, and the relationship between inputs and outputs may be completely different. Information and ideas, for example, are not used up in production but can be used over and over again. The quality of some services (for example, legal or medical advice) may matter much more than the quantity (the amount of time spent by the service provider). There may be "network" effects, or complementarities, that make a particular "product" (a computer operating system, for example) worth much more to one customer if others are using the same product or that make one product more valuable if it is used with another product than when used alone.

Relatedly, the innovation process has become much more complex. While the history of technological change is filled with stories of discrete inventions (the turbine engine, the electric light, penicillin), innovation is now almost continuous and imbedded in the production process itself. As recently as two decades ago, companies tended to conduct research as a separate operation, in a laboratory apart from the production operation. Today, in many companies research and development activities are integrated into production operations as part of their continuous efforts to improve both process and product.

These changes have been so transforming that the old language to describe how goods and services are produced and distributed often no longer seems to apply, and new models may seem outdated or inaccurate almost as soon as they are developed. As a result, the lack of clear, consistent, and robust definitions and the inherent difficulties of measuring many of the things that need to be measured are themselves an obstacle to better understanding. Sears, Roebuck Co., for example, has been trying to develop a model that would show a link from employee satisfaction to customer loyalty to profit. The company has spent more than five years refining its data capture mechanisms but has only recently been able to use its model to describe operations at the department level.[44]

The paucity of good robust models and consistent vocabulary for intangibles also stands in the way of development of performance or measurement data that would be comparable across firms. Moreover, any effort to develop comparable data is likely to be hampered by the "public goods" problem: even though it would be in everyone's interest to have better data, it is not in any single person's interest to expend the resources to collect and develop the data, especially if, once collected, the data would be made available to all. Public goods problems cannot be solved by individual participants in a market, but they can sometimes be overcome by some form of collective action. One possibility would be for a government agency, or government-sponsored agency, to help develop models and collect data. This solution would have both the advantages and disadvantages arising from the power of government to require firms to report certain kinds of data. Alternatively, private sector groups might form an association and agree to tax themselves or otherwise commit to contributing resources to develop appropriate models and collect the necessary data.

> *To overcome the public goods problem in developing models and data on intangibles, a government agency could be engaged, or private sector companies could form an association to do so.*

## Accounting Profession Concerns

Some members of the accounting profession in the United States have been wary of policymakers' concerns about the problem of measuring and reporting on intangible assets because of the historic commitment of the profession to the integrity and auditability of financial reports. Others have been pressing hard for both a policy debate and public policy solutions to this issue. In seeking to better understand the disparate views of the accounting profession, the SEC and Financial Reporting subgroup of the task force identified five broad perspectives on the problem, associated with the following groups: financial statement preparers, users of financial statement information in the investment community, auditors, standard setters, and regulators. Researchers met with representatives of the leading organizations representing these perspectives.[45] Of the concerns raised in these meetings, the most intense related to fears that measures of intangible inputs are inherently "soft," that they would be difficult to audit, and that including such information on the balance sheet would compromise the financial reporting process.[46]

Members of the accounting community have tended to regard conservative approaches to accounting as a virtue. The FASB notes that "historically, managers, investors, and accountants have generally preferred that possible errors in measurement be in the direction of understatement rather than overstatement of net income and assets. . . . [This] convention of conservatism . . . was once commonly expressed in the admonition to 'anticipate no profits but anticipate all losses.'" The FASB now officially recognizes that the bias imparted by a preference for the understatement of assets leads to a future bias toward overstatement of earnings, and that such biases are not necessarily beneficial. Nonetheless, the idea that the deliberate understatement of assets is a virtue is "deeply ingrained and is still in evidence despite efforts over the past 40 years to change it."[47]

Despite these concerns, or perhaps because of them, several key organizations within the profession have formed special committees or task forces to look into the reporting issues raised by intangibles investments, including the Financial Accounting Standards Board, the International Accounting Standards Committee (IASC), the American Institute of Certified Public Accountants (AICPA), and the Securities and Exchange Commission, which is the final arbiter of these issues in the United States.

**Business Community Concerns**    Although numerous corporations are trying to develop special measures and performance indicators as internal management tools, among corporate executives there is widespread resistance to increasing the *required* disclosure in this area. This aversion arises from at least four concerns:

*Measures are preliminary and experimental.* Most enterprises are still struggling with how to identify and measure intangibles for their own internal purposes. Executives realize that any measures they develop may change several times as they hone their understanding of the intangible factors that are important to performance, and that the results may therefore not be consistent over time.[48] Indeed, many measures used in individual firms may be useful primarily as indicators of progress toward specific goals, and once the goals are met, these data may not be worth collecting any more. Given the experimental nature of many metrics that are being tried, and the less than compelling evidence that these nascent measures can be directly linked to financial outcomes, it is not surprising that corporate executives would be reluctant to enshrine these experiments in permanent public disclosures.

*Disclosure could undermine competitive advantage.* To the extent that companies have been able to develop useful nonfinancial performance indicators, they are likely to feel that these indicators provide a competitive advantage and are proprietary information that they want to keep from their competitors. To assess the true growth of Internet retailers, for example, financial analysts have developed an indicator based on comparing total revenues for each quarter to total customer base. Retailers such as Amazon.com and CDNow have criticized this metric, pointing out that the denominator is cumulative and fails to distinguish between customers who visit once and frequent purchasers. Yet few companies have released the numbers that would provide a better measure of growth. Amazon.com, for example, could disclose how many customers it has each quarter, a statistic that would provide a fairer measure of growth. But it will not do so. "We consider it proprietary information," an Amazon spokesperson recently told the *New York Times*.[49]

*Executives fear legal liability.*   Under federal securities law, the officers and directors of a company, as well as those who prepare the company's financial statements, can be held personally liable for statements made to the public that are false or misleading with respect to any material fact.[50] As a result of this rule, corporate executives are wary of making forecasts about the potential of a planned or ongoing project because such forecasts could prove wrong and make the firm and its officers vulnerable to a lawsuit by unhappy shareholders. For similar reasons, corporate executives are often reluctant to talk about the value of intangible assets, because that value depends on the future cash flows that will be generated by the asset, which may be speculative. Although the Private Securities Litigation Reform Act of 1995 provided for somewhat greater protections for some kinds of forward-looking information, many executives still express reservations about these disclosures.[51] Until the business community perceives the risks of litigation to be slight, there will continue to be resistance to mandatory disclosure and reluctance to experiment with greater voluntary disclosure.

*Best presentation for public reporting purposes.* The recent controversy over the proper accounting treatment of mergers in the high-tech sector illustrates this problem. As noted above, under current accounting rules, which do not recognize the value of internally produced intangibles, mergers present a dilemma. A significant number of members of the accounting community believe that the purchase method should be applied to mergers, and in 1999 the FASB proposed a rule change that would require this treatment.[52] Under the purchase method, the acquiring firm adds the target firm's tangible and identifiable intangible assets to its books at market value and implicitly recognizes the value of the remaining acquired intangibles by adding a substantial amount of goodwill to its books at the time of the acquisition. But its own internally developed intangibles continue to be carried on the books at essentially zero value. As a result, the accounting treatment of intangible assets from different sources in the combined entity, as it were, mixes "apples" and "oranges."

Opponents have argued that purchase accounting adds to the accounting confusion, in contrast to the pooling method, in which the assets of the target firm are added to the acquired firm's books at book value. Under pooling treatment, the discrepancy between book value and market value of the surviving firm was increased by the transaction, but at least the internally developed intangibles of both original firms were treated in the same way—that is, ignored—in the combined entity.

Under purchase accounting, the acquired intangible assets are at least recognized on the books as assets. But the acquiring firm is subsequently required to take annual depreciation charges against operating earnings until that goodwill has been written off the books. The depreciation charges required under purchase accounting can result in a substantial drag on reported operating earnings in the years after a merger.

Firms such as Cisco Systems, for which acquisitions are an important method of growth, complained that financial markets would penalize them for having lower subsequent earnings performance if they were required to report the transactions under purchase accounting and take charges against earnings in the future, even when they believe there is no impairment of goodwill. Besides, they feel that the change would not add clarity to the information available to investors about the nature and value of their intangible assets. For these reasons, Cisco and other high-tech firms have lobbied hard to stop the FASB from changing its accounting rules.[53]

In response to these concerns, the FASB was expected to issue in early 2001 a new standard that would require firms making acquisitions—even stock-for-stock acquisitions—to account for those transactions on their books using the purchase method. But buyers will not be required to depreciate the acquired goodwill unless it becomes "impaired" (an accounting term meaning that the asset is worth less than is currently recorded on the firm's books). The criteria for determining whether the assets are impaired are left largely to the discretion of the buying company's management.

Finance theorists have long argued that accounting treatments such as those at stake in this debate should not affect the value that the financial markets assign to corporations because they are only book effects, not substantive changes in the reality of what the company is doing and how much cash flow it is generating. But corporate executives seem to believe that financial markets will not be able to see through the accounting treatment to the reality, and there is some empirical evidence to support their fears.[54]

More generally, firms are aware that additional disclosures can help them when the information is good, but can hurt them when the information is not so good. Hence the business community tends to be wary of changes that will commit them to any form of expanded disclosure.

**Investment Community Concerns**  Although one might think that those who make their living by investing in or trading corporate securities would be leading the charge for better information, a variety of factors have made investment analysts, traders, and institutional investors cautious about the idea that firms should develop and report more information on their investments in intangibles.

*Resistance to changing paradigms.*  Securities analysts who focus on fundamentals, as well as the so-called quants, who use complex quantitative models to assess value and make buy or sell recommendations, have generally learned to look at firms in certain ways and resist radically rethinking the tools they use, especially when the information available to them on intangible assets seems soft, or subjective, or unstable.[55] Their risk models and discounted cash flow models do not have the capacity to incorporate such information, and they do not have alternative models that they regard as theoretically sound or empirically tested. Moreover, most analysts have not had to worry much about intangibles until very recently. Financial analysts also have historically preferred conservative accounting rules. The Association for Investment Management Research, for example, has expressed serious reservations about the idea of capitalizing R&D.[56]

*Proprietary methods.* Some securities analysts, however, have developed their own models and metrics for assigning value to the intangible assets in firms. To the extent that their analyses lead to better forecasts and investing advice, they are likely to regard their valuation methods as a source of personal competitive advantage and to view them as proprietary. Thus they do not have an incentive to promote the standardization of information on intangibles and the enhanced public reporting of such information by firms.

*Selective access to information.* A final reason why many members of the financial community, especially analysts representing large financial institutions, have not been especially enthusiastic about or supportive of efforts to develop better performance indicators and enhanced disclosure requirements for publicly traded firms is that they have often had special access to corporate executives. Analysts representing large financial institutions would seek out and get special briefings, or call executives at companies with specific questions, or otherwise use their access to get the information they needed. In essence, these analysts, and the investor organizations they represent, were benefiting from selective disclosure, and they therefore had no incentive to encourage more systematic and formal forms of disclosure.

However, the SEC has been concerned about selective disclosure for some time, and, as described above, in August 2000 promulgated Regulation FD, which is intended to reduce some of this selective disclosure advantage. Critics of the new regulation argue that it may discourage corporations from releasing any information they are not required to disclose, or from meeting with analysts at all, except in very large public meetings.[57] But the relevant question for our purposes is whether the sporadic and voluntary disclosure of ad hoc information, either selectively as before, to analysts and institutions at their request, or more generally, to all investors, say, over the Internet, is an acceptable substitute for regular quantitative comparable and verifiable disclosure in a medium that can reach all investors at the same time. We believe not.

**Are the Barriers Insurmountable?** Many of the people most directly affected by the lack of good information on the role of investments in intangibles in the economy have been cautious about endorsing various efforts to address the problem—including many with quite principled and public-spirited objections. Nonetheless, as the discrepancy between what really matters for firms' performance and what they are reporting publicly increases, momentum is growing for some sort of broad-based public or private initiative to address this discrepancy through increased information gathering and reporting. Task force members believe that most of the objections of the various affected parties can be appropriately addressed and that in the long run the most significant barrier to better information is the lack of a clear or obvious model to guide the information gathering and reporting process. However, the short-term obstacles to the development of new reporting models of this type are formidable.

A recurring question for the task force had to do with the appropriate role for government in developing better information about and supporting investments in intangible assets. In a political environment where the prevailing ideology favors market solutions rather than government solutions to economic problems, many of us instinctively felt that the government should not attempt to develop new business models or determine what new measures and indicators of business performance would be most useful or informative in tracking such a rapidly evolving economy. The private sector is where the rubber meets the road, and many players in the private sector have powerful incentives to develop better performance measures. The private sector is also likely to have a better sense of how investment resources ought to be allocated.

Many of us suspected, however, that there were numerous public policies—including rules, regulations, and reporting requirements in a variety of different areas—that were put into place in a "hard-asset" world and might be less relevant or appropriate in a "soft-asset" world, particularly if they represented barriers to investment or to better measures of disclosure of intangibles. We therefore thought that it would be useful to survey the policy environment, looking for places where adjustments might be required to ensure that, to the extent possible, policies do not create a bias against investments in intangibles or inadvertently impede private sector efforts to develop better metrics for tracking intangibles and their contribution to the economy. On further reflection, it became clear that government policies are more deeply implicated in the creation and valuation of intangibles than we had at first realized. To fully address government's role in developing better measurement systems as well as in supporting intangibles investments, one must be mindful of government's role in creating intangibles in the first place.

# CHAPTER THREE

# The Role of Government

Many intangible assets are, in an important sense, the product of government policy. Intellectual property rights laws, as well as the laws that govern corporations, contracts, and labor relations, help to define which streams of benefits from which "assets" are protected as property, and who gets the benefit of that protection. In other words, many intangible assets would not exist as assets at all without the starting point of a set of property rights defined and guaranteed at the state or federal level.

*Many intangible assets would not exist as assets without the underpinning of property rights defined and guaranteed by the government.*

**Determining Property Rights**
The founding fathers understood the establishment of property rights as an important role for government and included in the Constitution a clause giving Congress the power "to promote the Progress of Science and useful Arts, by securing for limited Times to Authors and Inventors the exclusive Right to their respective Writings and Discoveries."[58] In 1790, Congress acted on this authority and enacted the first patent act. Thomas Jefferson was appointed as the first

"patent examiner."[59] A patent transforms an idea into a piece of property that the inventor can prevent others from using without his or her permission. A patent can also be transferred, sold, or licensed to others.

Nonpatented ideas that are in widespread use (the wheel, for example) may have enormous economic value, but most of this is captured in the tangible objects that incorporate these ideas. At the frontiers of knowledge, where technology is advancing rapidly, new ideas may have a great deal of value that has not yet been incorporated into tangible objects whose value can be estimated relatively easily. Once an intangible idea has been patented, however, the stream of economic benefits from that idea is assigned to a single individual (the patent holder), who can exploit and protect those benefits. This makes it somewhat easier to estimate its value. But whereas tangible property may be owned, or at least controlled, by someone or some entity as long as it exists, control rights over intangible assets exist only to the extent the government creates them. These rights are highly contingent, are generally harder to define, and are usually limited by law to a certain period of time.[60]

In addition to patents on inventions, the federal government also provides trademark protection, which makes it easier for businesses to create and build reputational capital. Similarly, federal copyright protections give authors, composers, playwrights, film makers, sculptors, and other artists exclusive property rights over their creations.[61] And both patent and copyright law can be used to transform computer software into protected property.

Moreover, state statutory and common law governing agency, contracts, corporations, and the relationships between an employee and an employer also help to determine who is entitled to the benefits from information, ideas, and business opportunities developed on the job or in the process of pursuing some collaborative business enterprise. Thus the whole legal framework of property, contract, and business law helps to determine what is "ownable"; who is entitled to capture the benefits of some idea, relationship, or opportunity; and how securely those benefits can be protected.

**Research and Setting Standards** Beyond creating, assigning, and protecting property rights over intangible assets, the federal government and most state governments have also been directly involved in the development of intangible assets through the funding of basic and applied research, the standardization of measurements, and the dissemination of knowledge.

The federal government has a long history of funding research and higher education, going back at least to the creation of the land grant university system in the mid–nineteenth century. The Morrill Act of 1862 channeled resources into the teaching of "agriculture and the mechanical arts," and the Hatch Act of 1887 provided resources for research into agricultural technology. Federal funding for research has continued since. As recently as 1998, federal, state, and local governments together funded as much as 67 percent of all academic research and 13 percent of all research carried out by industry.[62] In these ways, government has been quite influential in providing the fertile soil in which the private sector continues to cultivate and harvest intangible wealth in the early twenty-first century.

The federal government has also been actively involved in measurement and standards setting. Nearly a century ago, Congress created the National Bureau of Standards, now the National Institute of Standards and Technology (NIST), to support industry, commerce, and scientific institutions by providing research that helped set basic technical and physical standards for measurements (weight, time, temperature, materials) and testing. In recent years, NIST has also become involved in setting management and quality control standards through its participation in the administration of the Malcolm Baldridge National Quality Award program.[63]

Perhaps more relevant to the current debate over valuation and reporting of intangibles, the federal government has also played a key role in the standardization of accounting methods. The Securities Exchange Act of 1934 created the Securities and Exchange Commission, with the authority to prescribe accounting principles for public companies. The SEC has always relied on professional organizations to develop such principles, and because securities law requires that companies that issue and sell securities to the public publish regular financial reports in accordance with "generally accepted accounting principles," these private sector organizations have had enormous authority.[64]

Thus, while the task force believes that new business models better suited to describing and tracking an intangibles-driven economy are probably more likely to be developed by the private sector than by government fiat, we nonetheless recognize the fundamental role of government in the creation, measurement, disclosure, and reporting of intangible assets. We further believe that government could play an important role in solving the public goods or collective action problems associated with assembling the data necessary to develop and test new reporting models for the economy of the twenty-first century.

# CHAPTER FOUR

# Addressing the Problem of Measurement

The ultimate goal of measurement, accounting, and information reporting systems in business enterprises and at the levels of industries and the national economy is to enable executives and policymakers to make better resource allocation decisions. Are enough resources going into employee training and development relative to purchases of new equipment and software, for example? Are investors willing to put new capital into worthy new intangibles-intensive business ventures—at a reasonable cost of capital? Should government provide stronger tax incentives to encourage more investments in intangibles? Although all task force members recognized this goal, the resource allocation questions ultimately proved too difficult to address with specific recommendations, given the immensity of the information problems.

There was controversy within the task force over such basic questions as whether policy ought to be neutral, that is, neither encouraging nor discouraging investments in intangibles relative to tangible assets. While most of us support the principle of neutrality in general, some argued that many kinds of intangible assets provide substantial "spillover" benefits to parties other than those who make the investment to develop them. Numerous studies have shown that

R&D and employee training, for example, have spillover benefits, so that the benefit to society from investments in such intangibles far exceeds the

*Because intangible assets often provide substantial spillover benefits, many government policies are already tilted toward promoting certain kinds of intangible investments.*

benefit to the firm that makes the investments.[65] Most policy analysts agree that where there are spillover benefits from certain kinds of investments, efficiency can in theory be improved by government actions that promote such investments. In fact for just these reasons, many government policies, such as direct federal funding of research as well as tax incentives for corporate R&D, are already tilted toward promoting certain kinds of intangible investments.

Others on the task force felt that the level of knowledge about the role of most intangibles is too rudimentary to alter policy levers in an attempt to further shift the allocation of investment resources. "Any policy change now could shift the inequities and advantages that might currently exist without a clear and forward-looking understanding of the actions," concluded the Strategic Organizational Issues subgroup. "The downside risk of unintended consequences of policy change is too great."[66]

In this report, we make policy recommendations that we believe would support, enhance, and promote the development of new business reporting models that could better identify, measure, and monitor intangible assets. We do not suggest policy primarily intended to alter the allocation of investment resources. However, we do discuss several areas where existing policies that influence the allocation of investment resources deserve further research and study.

## Characterizing Measurement Problems

The task force subgroups encountered a wide range of difficulty in identifying and measuring intangibles, depending on the extent to which property rights over the intangibles were clear, or the nature of the intangibles was such that property rights could be assigned or clarified. Leif Edvinsson, former vice president and director of intellectual capital at Skandia AFS, took an early lead in developing extensive external reporting systems to describe and document intangible assets. He suggests that intangibles can be divided into "human capital" and "structural capital."[67] While "human capital is a critical component to the success of any company but one that walks out every evening," Edvinsson notes, "structural capital . . . is what's left in the company after the people go home. . . . it can be owned."[68] We make a similar distinction to identify three levels of measurement problems. At level 1 are assets that can be owned and sold. At level 2 are assets that can be controlled but not separated out and sold. At level 3 are intangibles that may not even be wholly controlled by the firm.[69]

> *We identify three levels of measurement problems for intangibles:*
> 1. *assets can be owned and sold*
> 2. *assets can be controlled but not separated out and sold*
> 3. *intangibles may not be wholly controlled by the firm*

### Level 1. Assets Can Be Owned and Sold

Patents, copyrights, brands, and trade names are examples of assets for which property rights are, to some extent, defined and protected by existing legal systems. There may not be perfect clarity about property rights over these intangibles, but at least they are considered "property" under current law.

If property rights are clear enough, the asset can be sold, and if an intangible asset or good has been purchased by or transferred to another party for consideration, that transaction provides an obvious, and useful, indicator of the value of the asset. An intangible asset that can be sold for consideration clearly meets the four accounting criteria for being recognized as an "asset" on the books of a company: it is well-defined and sufficiently separate from other assets that it can be the object of a sales transaction; the firm has effective control over it and can transfer that control to someone else; it is (reasonably) possible to predict the future economic benefits from it; and it is (reasonably) possible to determine if its economic value has been impaired.

*If an intangible asset can be sold for consideration, it clearly meets the four accounting criteria to be recognized as an "asset" — it is well-defined and separate from other assets — the firm has control over it and can transfer that control — the future economic benefits it will provide can be predicted — any impairment of its economic value can be determined*

In addition to intellectual property, other kinds of business agreements, executory contracts, licenses, and databases may appear to qualify as assets (or liabilities) for accounting purposes; for example, mailing lists, operating licenses and franchises, media and other broadcast licenses, agricultural and other production quotas in regulated industries, and employment contracts. But they are generally not included on the balance sheets of companies unless they have been the object of a transaction.[70]

If such assets are developed internally within a company, the expenditures associated with development are expensed immediately, and no asset is recorded. Income from the assets is treated as current income, but no depreciation charge is taken against it. If the assets are sold or transferred, the receipts from the transaction are recorded as a gain on sale, but there is no recognized reduction in balance sheet assets as a result of the sale. The firm that purchases the assets, however, will add the assets to its books. And if one firm buys another firm, and in so doing acquires a substantial bundle of such assets, the acquiring firm may add some goodwill to its balance sheet to reflect the difference between the price paid to acquire the firm and the estimated market value of the acquired firm's assets (after any allowable write-ups).

The task force believes that it should be possible to develop useful information about the costs incurred by firms in developing assets in this category, and probably also to develop information about the value of these assets. And there are strong reasons why such information should be made available to investors in a more consistent manner. In order to develop these types of information, several issues need to be resolved, including securing and clarifying property rights with respect to such assets, developing consistent rules for capturing information about the firm's expenditures in developing or acquiring the assets, and developing consistent, replicable appraisal techniques for assigning values to these assets. The third problem is most important for assets that have not yet been the object of a transaction. The business community's resistance to any disclosure requirements regarding such assets must also be addressed.

### Level 2. Assets Can Be Controlled But
### Not Separated Out and Sold

A more difficult set of problems arises in the attempt to identify, measure, and account for intangibles that are proprietary to a specific firm but would be very difficult to separate out and sell to another firm; for example, R&D in process, business secrets, reputational capital, proprietary management systems, and business processes. These intangibles may meet only one or two of the accounting criteria for "assets." The firm may have effective control over them—in that limited sense, the firm is understood to "own" the assets—and it may be possible to make some predictions about the economic benefits they provide. But it may not be possible to separate them out from other intangibles in the firm to determine their separate value or to convey them to some other party, unless they are bundled with the other factors to which they are tied.

The problems that must be solved in order to improve the flow of information about and management of assets at this level include all of the problems that apply to assets at level 1, and more. A consistent vocabulary must be developed for describing and defining such assets. Likewise, consistent and widely accepted business models must be constructed that can provide insight into how these assets interact with others in the firm to produce value. In some cases, it may be possible to provide stronger property rights protections for such assets, which would push them closer to level 1 and make it easier to assign them value. However, since the techniques for giving firms stronger property rights over such assets (such as providing additional protection for "business processes" and strengthening the enforceability of "noncompete" clauses in employment contracts) might have other, undesirable effects, it is not obvious that stronger property rights protections would be good public policy, even if they simplify the task of measuring, accounting for, and managing such assets.

### Level 3. Intangibles May not Be Wholly Controlled by the Firm

At this level are intangibles that have gone by such names as human capital, core competencies, organizational capital, and relationship capital. These "assets" (although they clearly do not meet any of the four accounting criteria) are inextricably tied up with the people who work for a firm and those who supply services or goods to the firm, such as consultants or networks of suppliers and others. The firm does not have legal property rights over these intangibles. There are at least two parties involved in the accumulation and utilization of human capital, for example: the employee and the firm. Investments in human capital differ from investments in tangibles, and even from investments in many categories of intangible assets, because workers can walk out the door at any time, taking their knowledge and skills with them. Although a firm may be able to prevent former employees from competing with it and thereby capitalizing on the knowledge or skills they took with them when they left, the firm cannot compel those employees to leave the knowledge and skills behind.

This does not mean that the firm has no influence over the development, retention, and utilization of such intangibles, however. In fact, a firm's personnel, management, and training policies may have a very large effect on the productivity, innovativeness, and profitability of a firm. And part of the value that gets recorded as goodwill in some corporate mergers may be due to such policies, rather than to level 1 or level 2 assets. Hence, even if it never becomes possible to "measure" such intangibles directly or add them to the books of the firm, managers inside firms and investors outside might want to know a great deal more about them than they currently do.[71] Moreover, one of the important tasks for management is to try to convert level 3 intangibles to level 2 or level 1 assets, for example, by codifying the knowledge of employees, or formalizing management procedures and decision tools, or asserting property rights over the laboratory notes of researchers.

The problems that must be solved to improve the flow of information about intangibles at this level include, in addition to all of those experienced at level 2, developing consistent vocabulary, definitions, and business models that can provide guidance about the relationships among investments in level 3 intangibles and other measures of performance in the firm.

# Improving Measurement and Reporting

Although the job is formidable, the task force feels strongly that progress can and should be made in developing better information about intangibles and their impact on the valuation of firms and on aggregate economic performance. We also believe that government has an important role to play in this effort. In this chapter we focus on two areas of potential government involvement. First, we propose a research agenda to be undertaken by a public-private partnership to develop better data about intangibles, especially level 2 and level 3 intangibles, such as R&D, organizational capital, and human capital. The ultimate aim of this project would be to create a resource that can be used by scholars and business practitioners to develop more useful business reporting models. Second, we recommend some immediate changes in financial reporting rules. In the next chapter we suggest some changes in intellectual property rights laws that would reduce the uncertainty around property rights in level 1 assets.

## R&D and Organizational and Human Capital

For intangibles that are recognizable as "assets," that can be bought and sold, and about which property rights are relatively clear, market information about their value may often be available or can be developed through appraisal techniques. But for what we have called level 2 and level 3 intangibles, the problems involved in identifying, describing, measuring, and tracking them and understanding their role in the evolution of the economy are more intractable. Most task force members began work with the suspi-

*Existing public policies are not the primary impediments to developing better information about the role of intangibles in the economy—the most important barriers are cognitive.*

cion that certain aspects of public policy might be exacerbating the inherent measurement difficulties. But after two years of study, most of us agreed that existing public policies are not currently the primary impediments to developing better information about factors such as in-process R&D, organizational capital, or human capital. The most important impediments, instead, are conceptual.

The cognitive problems begin with the fact that many of the factors relevant to the value of level 2 and level 3 intangibles are probably not directly measurable, because they cannot be clearly separated from other related factors. Thus the best one can hope for at present is to identify and develop indirect indicators, or clusters of indicators, to help understand the roles played by these factors in productivity and wealth creation, both at the level of the individual firm and at the aggregate level. But it is not clear what should be measured, let alone how to measure it. There is a chicken-and-egg quality to this problem: one needs better data to understand the changes going on in the New Economy and the dynamic relationships between investments in intangibles and economic performance. And to collect better data, one needs better business models and frameworks to guide the decision of what data to collect. But to develop better business models and frameworks, one needs better data.

Moreover, there seems to be a substantial public goods problem in trying to assemble the necessary data. It would be in the interest of virtually every firm to have better business information models (at least for its own internal use) and better industry or sector-specific performance information to feed into these models for benchmarking purposes. But because it is costly to develop such models and collect such data from a large enough sample of firms, no one firm, acting individually, has the incentive to undertake the task.

Some researchers have argued that markets will solve the problem of providing better information on intangibles without government assistance or regulation, because a firm should have an incentive to disclose a wider range of nonfinancial information in order to reduce financial markets' uncertainty about the value of its work, and thereby reduce its cost of capital.[72] We do not think this is likely to happen soon. Market incentives alone will probably not lead to the development of consistent, verifiable metrics and measurement standards because the costs associated with such development outweigh the potential reduction in the cost of capital for any one firm.

One can imagine hundreds of thousands of snippets of information that firms might selectively, and on their own initiative, provide to investors; for example, how many new products are under development, how many Ph.D.s they hired last year, improvement in customer satisfaction, cumulative number of hits on a website. But such information is just fog if it is not reported regularly and collected in a consistent and sensible way; one needs to determine how to define "new product," what was the net increase in Ph.D.'s counting departures as well as new hires, how is customer satisfaction measured, what proportion of the hits represent repeat customers and what proportion are new customers. Moreover, such data would also be vastly more informative if they could be compared to industry benchmarks that were also collected regularly and consistently.

*The public sector should provide financial support and coordinate the efforts of private sector players to overcome the public goods problem in developing regular, consistent, and comparable information about business investments in R&D, organizational capital, and human capital.*

Thus the task force concludes that there is a strong positive role for the federal government in solving this particular public goods problem. Uncoordinated and isolated efforts within the private marketplace will not achieve the necessary outcomes as swiftly or as well as if the public sector provides financial support and coordinates the efforts of private sector players. In particular, government should actively

— facilitate the convening of all interested stakeholders;

— help to finance the research necessary to monitor and evaluate experimentation in measurement and disclosure; and

— foster the promotion of voluntary guidelines that would increase the availability of comparable and verifiable information about business investments in R&D, in structural or organizational capital, and in human capital.

### Center for the Study of Business, Technology, and Innovation

We propose the creation of a new, federally funded Center for the Study of Business, Technology, and Innovation. The center would be a collaboration between government and the private sector, drawing on expertise from the Bureau of Economic Analysis at the Department of Commerce, the Center for Economic Studies at the Bureau of the Census, the Bureau of Labor Statistics, the National Science Foundation, private sector organizations such as the Conference Board, the American Institute of Certified Public Accountants or other representatives of the accounting profession, and corporate opinion leaders.[73] At least initially, the center should perhaps be housed at the Bureau of Economic Analysis, which is already in the business of assembling data on the national accounts, or at the Center for Economic Studies, which already has a massive collection of plant-level business data and an established reputation in the business community for handling data with confidentiality.

The immediate goals of the center's research should be to develop a more comprehensive set of macroeconomic and microeconomic performance indicators that could better track developments in the New Economy and to provide useful industry-level information to individual firms for benchmarking purposes. The longer-term goal would be to help establish standards for expanded reporting by publicly traded firms and an improved flow of information to investors making capital allocation decisions. Hence the Financial Accounting Standards Board and the Securities and Exchange Commission should closely monitor the work of the center and the research that it produces. As reliable, auditable, and verifiable performance indicators are developed, these agencies should consider whether they should be included in the disclosures required of publicly traded companies, and if so, how and in what form. In the meantime, publicly traded firms should be given greater latitude and regulatory protection for increased voluntary disclosures (see discussion below).

As a first step toward the creation of such a center, a pilot study should be set up to address the issues of data collection, designing a framework of value indicators, and developing new business models. Congress should provide funding for the pilot study; the Bureau of Economic Analysis, the Bureau of Labor Studies, the Census Bureau, and the National Science Foundation should jointly sponsor or otherwise support it; and the voluntary cooperation of some 100 to 150 private sector firms in at least a dozen different sectors of the economy should be enlisted over a three to four year period.

*Capturing a richer base of cost data on intangible investments.* Researchers would develop a template for collecting and reporting information about corporate investments that are directed at building specific intangible assets over time. The information structure should be capable of delineating the key asset-building outlays that currently flow through the traditional reporting system as periodic expenses. These might include, for example, breakouts of expenditures on basic research, new product development, on-going product and process improvement, the expenditures associated with quality assurance programs and service functions, training systems, the development and installation of information technology systems, advertising or brand development, market alliances, distribution networks, the enhancement and renewal of workforce skills, and salaries, bonuses, and incentive compensation systems.

Participating firms would work with the researchers to develop the data collection templates and to modify them as appropriate.[74] They might also be given modest grants to help defray the costs of developing the information capture systems within their firms and reporting back on just how costly those systems turn out to be, both to install and to operate. Participating firms should also receive feedback from the project (maintaining the confidentiality of the individual firm-level information) that would allow them to compare and rank their performance against each other.

*Developing a coherent framework of value indicators.* It is widely understood that, with intangibles perhaps even more than with tangible assets, the value created by an expenditure on developing the intangible may bear little relation to the cost. So in addition to capturing more cost information, the pilot project should develop a template for tracking the intermediate outcomes of prior investments in intangibles. The kind of information collected might include the number of patents or copyrights; patent licensing revenues; citation counts (as indicators of how influential the patents or copyrights proved to be); income from new products (for example, those introduced within the last three years); royalty in- and outflows; details about insourced and outsourced services; product life-cycle and time-to-market; growth and expansion of market share; and details about human resource management systems. Again, participating firms and other private sector organizations should work with researchers, advising them of indicators they feel are relevant to performance in their industries or sectors.

*Developing a new generation of business models.* During the first few years of the project, while the initial rounds of data are being collected, researchers should work with participating firms to develop and test models that more accurately describe the relationships among the various input and outcomes measures and to link the primary inputs to intermediate inputs and, ultimately, to financial performance and other measures of total value creation.

An example of the kind of reform needed is improvement in the standard protocols used to collect R&D information. Survey work by the Bureau of Economic Analysis, the National Science Foundation, and the Census Bureau, have been based on the concepts and definitions developed by the Organization for Economic Cooperation and Development (OECD).[75] Although these protocols have been updated several times—most recently in the fifth edition of the "Frascati manual" in 1994, with a further revision underway for release in 2002—they are widely perceived not to have kept pace with the changing scope and nature of R&D. Few organizations currently use the Frascati manual internally for their day-to-day operations.[76]

The Frascati definitions are based on a laboratory model of R&D and do not relate well to the profile of expenditures on R&D-related activities in most business firms today. The narrow, science-based definitions need to be adapted, for example, to make finer distinctions among innovation activities relating to basic research, near-market development, process re-engineering, and training and distribution, as well as to take account of the very different practices that have grown up in different industrial sectors, especially the service industries. As more data are collected, the new models being developed and tested as part of this pilot project should be continuously refined.

Although the underlying data collected in the pilot project would have to remain confidential, researchers should be encouraged to publish reports on a variety of aspects of the project, from the development of the data collection templates to the development and testing of the models. These reports and papers should be submitted to scholarly journals for publication, so they can be critiqued and evaluated by nonparticipant scholarly researchers. In addition, scholars who are given access to pilot project data for their research should be prohibited from exploiting them for commercial purposes.

Another major role for the center in its early years would be to collect information about and monitor efforts to experiment with new business reporting systems by private sector companies in the United States and by firms and governments in other countries. Some companies are already providing expanded, if somewhat ad hoc, information on topics such as social and environmental practices; recruiting, training and employee development programs; or incentive compensation programs intended to retain and motivate key people.[77] Some are publishing addenda to their annual reports, intellectual capital accounts, or reports to society.[78] These documents contain not only narrative accounts that explain how the organizations define and meet their ethical responsibilities to employees, suppliers, customers, owners, communities, and governments, but also metrics that help to hold the organizations to a standard of performance over time. In addition, in Europe a number of projects are under way to develop better reporting models for intangibles; examples include initiatives by the Danish government, the European Commission, the OECD, the Coalition for Environmentally Responsible Economies, and the Centre for Tomorrow's Company.[79] The Center for the Study of Business, Technology, and Innovation should open channels of communication and exchange information with international and private sector organizations such as these.

**Financial Reporting** Beyond improving firms' internal information and improving the understanding of aggregate economic performance, our sights are set on providing more reliable and useful information to financial markets, to guide the capital allocation decisions made by investors. Hence the task force also considered a number of questions about appropriate standards and protocols for public disclosure. There was no dispute that current disclosure rules are inadequate and that additional disclosures are vital if the public perception of fairness, transparency, and integrity in U.S. financial markets is to be maintained.[80] The problem is how to get from here to there.

As noted earlier, the Securities and Exchange Commission has elected to execute its responsibility for setting accounting standards for publicly held companies largely by monitoring the pronouncements of the Financial Accounting Standards Board. Consequently, any change in financial accounting requirements engages both the SEC and the FASB, although the SEC has complete authority and direct responsibility to promulgate reporting and disclosure requirements outside of the financial statements.

### Capitalizing versus Expensing

Under generally accepted accounting principles in the United States, expenditures on purchased patents, copyrights, and other intangibles are recorded as investments, whereas expenditures to develop these assets internally are treated as current expenses. One way to begin to reconcile this discrepancy in the accounting treatment would be to also "capitalize" expenditures on internally generated R&D (a level 2 intangible that, in some instances, involves generating level 1 assets in the form of patents), that is, treat them as investments in new assets. In recent years there has been intense debate over this issue in the accounting community, with proponents arguing that capitalization of R&D would improve the overall quality of balance sheet information by adding level 1 assets as they are being developed internally, and opponents arguing that, given the uncertainty associated with R&D projects, treating them as investments before it is known whether they are successful would be misleading and even more confusing.[81]

After some internal debate and extensive interviews with individuals preparing financial statements, users, auditors, standards setters, and regulators, the task force has concluded that the debate about capitalization versus expensing of R&D focuses on the wrong problem.[82] What investors want and need is information about the value of internally developed intangibles and the other factors that drive the value creation process in firms. They might also want cost information, so that they can evaluate the return a firm is getting on the dollars it spends on R&D and other programs. But it is irrelevant whether such information is incorporated into the regular financial statements of companies or presented in some other format, for example, in footnotes or the management discussion and analysis or in some other supplementary disclosure material. As long as the information is made available, it appears that investors are able to process and make use of it. In fact, most members of the task force concluded that capitalization of R&D, or any other intangibles, is a poor proxy for the richer information disclosure that we believe is necessary.

The only immediate change in required disclosure about intangibles in corporate financial statements unanimously agreed on by the task force is expanded breakout of cost information by type of expenditure at the business segment level.[83] This would at least increase the amount and detail of cost information available to investors.

### Move To a Value-Based Model

Users of financial information have made it clear that what really matters to them is the value of intangibles in a firm (rather than the cost of acquiring or developing them) and what are the so-called value drivers that will help to produce future cash flows.[84] Therefore the accounting profession in general, and the FASB in particular, should participate in a process of developing better internal valuation systems so that the financial reporting model can begin to move toward a value-based system of accounting for corporate assets—both tangibles and intangibles—that would supplement the current cost-based system.

Currently, internal efforts to track values of intangibles once the expenditures have been made range from non-existent to nascent. Moreover, many of those who have tried have found that attempts to value individual intangible assets—particularly at levels 2 or 3—have not so far been very fruitful. But we believe that it is possible to develop performance indicators that would add considerably to the cost-based information currently prepared and presented in financial statements. Hence the task force strongly encourages the FASB and the accounting profession to participate (as observers and advisers) in the data and model development project proposed above.

### Encourage Disclosures about Value Drivers

Formal disclosures in the public documents that firms must file with the SEC should include substantially more information than is currently provided on the factors that drive value in firms. Since there are not yet standard models or reporting protocols for such additional information, firms should be encouraged to use the management discussion and analysis section of the 10-K report to explain what management believes the value drivers are, how they are changing, and how the company is responding. For example, any large discrepancies between the book and market value of a firm's securities should be noted, and the value drivers that might account for that discrepancy identified.[85] Management should also present a discussion of the firm's strategy, with sufficient detail to provide a meaningful framework for evaluating the discussion of value drivers.

FASB Statement 131 establishes the regular review by the firm's chief operating officer as an important element in identifying reportable segments. We add to this principle the idea that the regular review should indicate that management has a perception about the underlying drivers that create value in the reviewed segments. Such information might be included in the segment footnote, for example.

A number of business consulting groups and academic researchers have proposed models for reporting nonfinancial information that may be quite useful for these purposes in particular situations.[86] Although the task force does not endorse any of these particular models for general use, we applaud the efforts being made by numerous players in the private sector and urge the SEC to monitor these initiatives and encourage experimentation in public reporting. These models should also provide useful starting points to researchers at the statistical agencies working on the data development project proposed above.

Some researchers have suggested that new developments in information management technology may make it possible and attractive for firms to make large amounts of raw data about operations and performance available online, for investors or others to collect, compile, assess, and interpret on their own.[87] Such technology is already being used to enable suppliers to receive instant information about their customers' sales and inventory levels, for example. We are enthusiastic about the potential of computer technology to reduce firms' costs of capturing data, as well as distributing and analyzing it. But for the time being we view these technological developments primarily as a means to facilitate experimentation and data building (by making it less costly for firms to participate in the data collection project proposed above, for example). Besides, corporations are not currently ready or willing to provide raw data in real time to investors, and in any event, models, analysis, valuation protocols, and protocols for collecting and verifying data would have to be developed first.[88]

### Expand Safe Harbor Protections

An important impediment to greater disclosure in the current system of securities regulation and financial reporting is managers' fear that if they attempt to describe or discuss "soft variables"—the intangible factors that they believe to be value drivers—or to assess the value implications of a company's strategy or efforts to develop intangibles, they might create a liability for the company to lawsuits if the realized values do not meet their reported expectations. As discussed briefly above, the 1995 Private Securities Litigation Reform Act provides some additional protection against lawsuits for firms that provide forward-looking information, but many business executives feel that it is insufficient.

The task force believes that a stronger safe harbor that would permit companies to experiment with additional disclosures is in order. We propose that a separate part of the Form 10-K be earmarked for disclosures that are specifically designated as experimental and inherently subject to mistakes and volatility. We further recommend that firms making such disclosures should be protected from legal liability at the federal level (with preemption at the state level), as long as the disclosure was made in good faith. We are convinced that the possible economic benefits of more and better information would outweigh the possibility that in some instances some investors would place too much weight on information that later proved to be inaccurate.

# CHAPTER SIX

# Improving Intellectual Property Rights Protection

A s discussed above, one of the most important ways that existing government policy influences the creation and valuation of intangibles is through legal protections for intellectual property rights. Once an intangible good has been defined by the law as a piece of property, and the rights associated with that property have been delimited, it becomes easier to estimate a value associated with those property rights and to sell, or transfer, or enter into other transactions involving that piece of property. Hence anything that increases certainty or clarity in laws that determine the scope, nature, and enforceability of intellectual property rights should make it easier to assign a value to the intellectual asset in question. This chapter identifies several problem areas in current intellectual property rights law and recommends changes to existing laws and legal systems that should provide a greater degree of certainty about rights in intangible assets.[89]

Intellectual property may be difficult to evaluate for several reasons, including factors that are specific to the owner of the property. For example, someone who acquires intellectual property rights but does not actively license and enforce them will surely realize less value from the intellectual property than would an owner who did. And an owner

73

of intellectual property who actively seeks out infringing parties for the purpose of soliciting licenses or settlement agreements may incur far greater costs in intellectual property protection and enforcement than an owner who does not. An owner who can effectively exclude competitors so as to become dominant in a large profitable market, however, can achieve significant value. These issues are considered by companies in developing strategies for managing intellectual property and, when relevant to valuing that property, should be disclosed and discussed in their public documents. Although these issues are important, they are separate from questions about the operation of the intellectual property laws and systems that are discussed in this section.

Our recommendations on intellectual property law focus primarily on the United States. Recognizing the ever-increasing significance of the global economy and marketplace, however, and the exponential growth of the Internet as a medium for communicating and for conducting business, we also make some proposals on international law.

**Patents**   While the establishment of the Court of Appeals for the Federal Circuit (CAFC) in 1982 has resulted in greater certainty and predictability of patent rights by funneling all patent disputes through a single appellate court of review, an additional step is needed to increase certainty and predictability in patent rights at the courts of first instance, the trial courts. The task force therefore recommends the establishment of a specialized trial court to preside over patent cases. This could be accomplished through a single court with judges sitting for trials in various parts of the country, or alternatively, each circuit could have specialized patent judges who handled all such cases in that circuit.[90]

It could be argued that specialized judges might be, or be perceived to be, too "propatent," in the sense of being predisposed to recognize the validity or infringement of patents brought before them. We believe, on the contrary, that a panel of specialized judges would become de facto experts in U.S. patent law issues and would therefore be more likely to bring a clear understanding of both the technical and the legal issues to the task. The result should be a fairer, speedier resolution of patent-related cases and controversies.

Another area of uncertainty and unpredictability in patent rights arises from the fact that patent laws vary from country to country. Today's borderless marketplace, a product of the expansion of electronic commerce associated with the Internet, demands that territoriality of patent rights must also be broadened. To that end, we recommend the establishment of an "international patent" that would harmonize international patent laws and provide patent owners with identical rights of exclusion in all countries that are signatories to the agreement.[91]

Given the logistical and political difficulties of establishing an international patent, for the short term we propose a "regional patent," which would extend the territoriality of patents for a smaller geographical area. A "North American Free Trade Agreement patent," for example, would have uniform effect within NAFTA member countries. Indeed, the European Union has already moved in this direction with the establishment of the European Patent Office, which issues EPO patents. Harmonization of international patent laws must be addressed by

*A specialized patent trial court should be established in the United States. And an international patent system should be created to extend the territoriality of patent rights in the global marketplace.*

the World Intellectual Property Organization (WIPO), working with the U.S. Congress and the executive branch of the U.S. government, especially the U.S. Trade Representative.

### Patenting Business Methods

The CAFC's decision in the 1998 case *State Street Bank & Trust Co.* v. *Signature Financial Group, Inc.* has been interpreted by the intellectual property community as removing barriers that might have existed to obtaining a patent on a so-called business method.[92] Since the decision was handed down, numerous patent applications have been filed that seek to protect methods of doing business. The Federal Circuit has recently reaffirmed its position that business methods are patentable subject matter in *AT&T Corp.* v. *Excel Communications, Inc.,* but the Supreme Court has not yet directly addressed the issue.[93]

There are two categories of business method patents. The first involves cases in which a specific method for achieving some business-related goal is implemented via software running on a computer system; for example, a specialized inventory-tracking system. The second category involves strictly conceptual or strategic business plans that have no reliance on any specialized computer- or software-based operation. In most of the Federal Circuit decisions addressing business method patents, the specific facts involved software; therefore, there is still speculation as to whether all types of business methods—including, for example, corporate business models and methods of providing services—will be found to be patentable subject matter.

Even prior to the *State Street Bank* decision, some of these methods of doing business might have been eligible for protection under trade secret laws. And those who argue that these business methods should remain an exception to patentable subject matter point to the vast field of state-level trade secret laws available in such cases. Patenting, however, generally provides stronger protection to the holder of the idea than is afforded to the owner of a trade secret.[94]

The patenting of business methods may also serve one of the important goals of the task force: the development and dissemination of better information about the role of intangibles in the economy. Nonetheless, we are cautious about this development in the law. We recommend that Congress and the Patent and Trade Office (PTO) monitor the issuance of business method patents over the next few years to assess the types of patents being granted, the additional burden on the courts, the impact on businesses, and the value of the additional information that patenting makes available to the market. Consistent with this recommendation, the PTO has recently instituted additional review procedures on business method patents.

**Trademarks**    In the United States, state common law rules regarding territorial trademark rights were incorporated into federal trademark law under the Lanham Act.[95] Federal registration of a mark provides nationwide rights in the protected mark and constructive notice to potential users of that mark in commerce, thus prohibiting independent duplication of a registered mark or "innocent use" by unauthorized users. But federal registration does not provide constructive notice to the user of a duplicate mark outside the United States.[96] The lack of global protection for trademarks adds to the uncertainty surrounding the value of this type of intangible asset.

The task force would like to see the United States take the initiative in working with other countries to develop a centralized international registration system for trademarks.

We recognize the enormous political difficulties in such a task—it took the United States one hundred years to sign on to the Berne Convention on Copyrights. But because the rapidly growing use of the Internet in international trade is quickly raising the stakes in this matter for many businesses both within and outside the United States, there may now be a window of political opportunity to open discussion in international forums, focusing first on the protection of trademarks used on the Internet. Hence, if necessary, as a first step toward the longer-term goal of broader protection for trademarks used in international trade, we propose that an international registration system be established for trademarks used on the Internet ("Internet trademarks").

This registration system would supplement current national trademark rights and registrations. That is, each country that takes part in the centralized registration of Internet trademarks will maintain its sovereignty within its own borders. However, anyone from a participating country who wishes to post a mark on the Internet will be charged with having constructive notice of all other specially registered marks being used on the Internet. Initially, the resulting trademark protection would apply only to the use of marks on the Internet. Moreover, rights in an Internet trademark should be renewable, as for all trademarks under U.S. trademark law, so that rights are protected as long as the mark is in use on the Internet and as long as the owner polices the mark. Internet domain names may be registered with various organizations, but such names alone, unless independently used as trademarks, would not be afforded Internet trademark status.

Closely related to the misappropriation of trademarks is the problem of "cybersquatting." Cybersquatters are those who register a domain name knowing that it copies or imitates the trademark of some other party. Typically, the expectation is that the owner of the trademark will be forced to pay a substantial fee to the registrant in order to purchase the domain name containing its trademark. A variant on this practice involves registering a domain name that is confusingly similar to a famous trademark (a common misspelling, for example), either to divert business from the trademark owner to the registrant or to confuse consumers into believing they have found the trademark owner's website. Cybersquatting has become a huge problem, and given the profits that have sometimes been made, it is not surprising that many have joined the game.

In order to address this problem, Congress passed the Anti-cybersquatting Consumer Protection Act, which went into effect in November 1999. In addition to prohibiting unauthorized individuals from registering domain names that imitate or include a trademark of some other party, the statute prohibits attempts to divert customers in a way that could harm the goodwill of a trademark. The task force supports this legislation and is optimistic that it will alleviate the problems associated with cybersquatting.

Furthermore, a procedure has been put in place through WIPO that makes it possible for one party to challenge the registration of a particular domain name by another party. This procedure results in an arbitration-like process. The current expectation is that this will greatly reduce the problem of cybersquatting internationally, but it may not eliminate it. Consequently, we believe that cybersquatting practices should be monitored internationally. If they continue to be a problem, the international community should be engaged in developing and enforcing stronger laws and procedures to contain cybersquatting.

## Implementing an Internet Trademark System

The following recommendations of the subgroup on Intellectual Property provide additional detail about how an Internet trademark protection system might be implemented.

The World Intellectual Property Organization should be the centralized registration body for Internet trademarks and the adjudicating body for all related disputes. Conflicts between domain names and trademarks should be resolved prior to registration of Internet trademarks with WIPO, through the Internet Corporation for Assigned Names and Numbers (ICANN) process. Transitional procedures should also be employed to minimize the potential risk of a rush-to-file phenomenon. For example, there should be an initial phase-in period of about two years after WIPO begins registering trademarks. During that period, owners of existing trademarks registered in the United States and abroad would have a prior claim on their marks as Internet trademarks, and other parties would not be able to appropriate those marks by registering them with WIPO. Upon expiration of the phase-in period, however, any party could register any mark for use on the Internet, as long as no one else had previously registered the mark with WIPO.

Critics of the establishment of what is, in effect, a separate jurisdiction for regulating trademarks used on the Internet argue that there is no need to treat cyberspace as a separate territory, with a set of rules governing trademarks separate and distinct from that used within an individual nation. Just as current U.S. law allows for similar trademarks to be used simultaneously when there is no likelihood of confusion about the source of the product or service identified by the mark, Internet trademarks could also be governed by territorially based laws. Factors such as price, accessibility, consumer preference, and type of goods would, according to this line of reasoning, define and segregate online markets just as offline markets have been segregated by the courts.

Certainly, de facto segregated virtual marketplaces have developed and will continue to develop on the Internet, with borders defined not by geography, but rather by the purposes, inclinations, and preferences of their users. The same mark might be used to identify two very different products sold on the Internet, for example, sheet rock and slippers. Nonetheless, we believe that the international registration of trademarks used on the Internet will greatly increase the certainty and predictability of the owners' rights in those marks. Moreover, it could be an important first step toward international acceptance of the need for broader international trademark protection.

**Trade Secrets**  "Trade secrets" is a concept developed at common law in order to provide a remedy to those who have been economically injured due to the improper disclosure to competitors of secrets or other specialized information used in conducting business. The earliest trade secret laws were based upon such theories as breach of fiduciary duty or breach of implied contract. Needless to say, the laws governing trade secrets have varied greatly from state to state.

Over the years a number of attempts have been made to harmonize the various state laws. But because the states are under no obligation to adopt any of the proposed model laws, state laws continue to vary considerably. In the 1970s the National Conference of Commissioners on Uniform State Laws again tried to harmonize state laws by drafting the Uniform Trade Secrets Act (UTSA). The UTSA has not been adopted by all state legislatures, however; at least forty have done so, but some have amended it to such a degree as to defeat the drafters' hopes of providing a uniform trade secret law. [97] A problem that arises from the lack of uniformity across states, and that contributes to uncertainty in the protection of property rights in trade secrets, is the phenomenon called "forum shopping," whereby litigants choose the state in which they sue. Naturally, they select the state with laws most sympathetic to the facts of their case.

The task force recommends that Congress enact a "Federal Trade Secret Act" (FTSA), by virtue of its authority under the Commerce Clause. Further, Congress should consider the UTSA as a starting point in drafting the federal law. The act would preempt inconsistent state laws under the Supremacy Clause and provide a high degree of certainty and predictability with regard to the legal treatment of trade secret cases. At the very least, it would put an end to forum shopping. That alone would increase the stability of trade secret rights, inasmuch as all litigants would know the law that would be applied to the facts and would presumably be more likely to settle. We also suggest that the field of trade secrets be revisited at some predetermined time after the enactment of a Federal Trade Secret Act, with the understanding that there will be room for improvement. After three to five years, for example, there would be ample evidence to show how the case law has interpreted the act. Moreover, this would provide an opportunity to further harmonize trade secret laws on a larger scale. The investigating body might consider harmonizing the act with the trade secret laws of other nations—perhaps enact an "International Trade Secret Treaty"—in much the same way as proposed above for patent law.

*Congress should enact a Federal Trade Secret Act that would preempt inconsistent state laws and provide a high degree of certainty and predictability in the enforcement of trade secret rights. But whether strong trade secret protection or weak protection encourages innovation and economic growth more is a question for further research.*

We do not make any specific recommendations about substantive trade secret law at this time. We note, however, that theory is undecided as to whether innovation and economic growth are encouraged more by strong trade secret protection or by weak protection. Hence, we emphasize that the scope of protection provided by any such federal law will need to be carefully considered in light of the theoretical and empirical controversies.

**Copyrights**    Copyrights enjoy the greatest degree of certainty and predictability of all the forms of intellectual property considered here.[98] The principal reason for the stability of copyright laws in the United States today is undoubtedly the fact that, since 1989, this country has been a signatory member of the Berne Convention.

Although copyrights are territorial and exist within the borders of a particular country, under the Berne Convention a territorial copyright automatically receives protection in all other member countries, according to the laws of the country where the infringement took place. When the copyright of a book first published in another country is infringed within U.S. borders, for example, that copyright, although of foreign origin, is conferred all the protections of a U.S. copyright under U.S. law.[99] This consistent treatment of copyrighted works within individual member countries, coupled with the fact that all member nations are required to make their own substantive copyright laws comply with certain minimum standards, has resulted in the relative uniformity of international copyright laws.

# CHAPTER SEVEN

# Policies Affecting Resource Allocation

The task force considered a number of areas where existing public policies probably influence the allocation of resources between tangible and intangible investments. But since intangibles themselves, and their role in the economy, are so poorly understood, we concluded that we could not make specific recommendations about any changes in policy as it affects resource allocation. Nonetheless, we call attention to some areas that merit further research into the implications of existing policies for the economy of the twenty-first century.

**Taxation** The Tax Policy subgroup concluded that tax policies per se do not present any direct impediment to the measurement or valuation of intangibles. Although for tax accounting purposes companies treat expenditures on internally developed intangibles as if they were current expenses rather than long-term investments, they are free to keep separate books for financial reporting purposes. So the tax rules do not, by themselves, interfere with the firm's ability to understand and account for the true nature of the expenses and their implications for value creation in the firm.

Tax policies clearly influence the allocation of investment resources, however. In general, tax rules tilt in favor of investments in intangibles relative to tangibles. Because spending on internally developed intangibles is immediately expensed, it represents a deduction from current income— and a corresponding reduction in immediate tax liability for profitable firms—of the full amount of any outlay incurred in a given year in connection with any internally developed intangible asset. By contrast, if a firm expends resources on a long-lived tangible asset, such as a new factory, a fleet of trucks, or new computer hardware, the firm capitalizes the expense in the current period and then takes a series of depreciation charges against income over several years.[100]

Thus a firm with growing investments in intangibles will report and pay taxes on lower income than a firm that makes the same outlays on tangible assets. It should be noted, however, that this effective deferral of tax liabilities is not a result of a deliberate policy to promote investment in intangibles but is simply due to the fact that, in general, internally developed intangibles are not recognized as long-lived assets for tax purposes.

Tax policies also influence intangibles investments in direct ways, for example, through R&D tax credits. Since 1981, Congress has provided special incentives to firms to encourage R&D activity. Firms that increase their amount of R&D activity relative to some base period are given a tax credit based on a complex formula that has changed from time to time. Expenses that qualify for this tax credit are defined narrowly—for example, they must be incurred in a research or experimentation activity designed to discover technological information about a new product, service, or production process—and over the years there has been considerable controversy over which expenses qualify.[101]

Some members of the task force felt that there is a strong case for government policy to be neutral, if possible, and that tax policy should not bend either toward or against encouraging investments in intangibles. From a purely theoretical perspective, there is no reason for taxes to favor one kind of investment relative to another if both produce the same social returns. But a number of task force members felt strongly that investments in intangibles should be tax-favored because they often provide substantial positive spillover effects. As noted above, spillover effects result from the fact that knowledge gained from R&D, for example, may not remain proprietary to those who have made the investment in this activity and may therefore benefit other parties. Thus the social returns from R&D are generally higher than the private returns. But because investors only consider their own private benefits and not the spillover benefits to the parties who made use of the knowledge, there would be too little investment in R&D relative to its social value without some biases that encourage R&D.

Among economists who study tax policy, the idea of using tax incentives to correct for this kind of market failure is not controversial. The difficulty comes in measuring the social benefits associated with different intangible investment activities—an issue that goes to the heart of the measurement problems on which this report focuses. Given the current state of knowledge about intangibles, we were not able to resolve the question of whether current tax policy provides the "right" amount of incentive. As more is learned about the role played by intangibles in the economy, further

> *Tax rules clearly influence the allocation of investment resources toward intangibles relative to tangibles. Many on the task force feel strongly that investments in intangibles should be tax-favored because of the substantial spillover effects.*

research should be done on the impact of tax policy on the allocation of resources.

**Capital Markets** The subgroup studying the impact of capital market institutions and regulations on intangibles concluded that there are no biases arising from capital market regulations or the procedures and credit standards used by lenders and other investors that, by themselves, impede development of better information about intangibles. But there is reason to believe that businesses based on intangible assets have more difficulty obtaining credit or raising equity capital (although as recently as mid-2000 this seemed not to be the case), particularly at the early stages of development, than do those based on tangible assets.

To be sure, lenders, including banks and insurance companies, and their regulators, consistently reported that their rules and standards for evaluating creditworthiness do not discriminate against borrowers whose assets are primarily intangible rather than tangible. They noted that credit risk does not depend on the nature of the assets: neither intangible assets nor bricks-and-mortar assets have intrinsic value if they are not useful for something. Thus, they insisted, it is the characteristics of an entity's cash-flow generation that determines the amount of credit it should receive.[102]

The bias in the credit markets, if there is one, arises because credit is generally unavailable to firms of any kind, regardless of the nature of their assets, until their cash flow characteristics have been established. But, especially with intellectual property–based businesses, the heavy funding needs come earlier in the process, and when assets that can be collateralized have not yet been created or acquired. This means that intangibles-intensive new businesses are, in general, much more heavily dependent on equity capital than bricks-and-mortar businesses.

The Capital Markets subgroup researched the sources of equity financing and concluded that a case might be made that some imbalances and frictions in the capital markets are impeding the flow of finance to small firms in the early stages of intangibles-intensive projects.[103] However, in light of the vibrant venture capital and initial public offering (IPO) market in the United States at the time of the task force's initial review, we did not believe that a compelling case then existed to conclude that there were systematic problems. As noted above, for example, a number of financiers had even begun buying securities backed by intellectual property assets. However, times change. As this report was going to press, seed financing and venture financing was extremely hard to come by, and many businesses previously founded and financed were going out of business because of a lack of capital to continue operations. Consequently, we believe this issue needs and merits further study. We also believe that many of the recommendations we make here would assist in ensuring that capital flows more evenly in the years ahead to those who deserve it.

**Federal R&D**   Federal policies relating to R&D probably influence the aggregate allocation of resources toward investments in intangibles and undoubtedly have interesting and complex implications for overall economic performance. The R&D Policy subgroup considered a number of issues associated with the shift in the allocation of federal R&D dollars from defense and space research to biotech research in recent years; the privatization of the knowledge acquired as a result of federal R&D spending, due to the fact that universities and individual scholars may obtain patents on such knowledge; and the education and training of science researchers and other Ph.Ds. Important though they are, the task force did not have sufficient empirical evidence about these issues to draw specific conclusions.[104]

# CHAPTER EIGHT

# Conclusions

The United States has the most transparent financial markets in the world. And in the past decade it has also been the fastest growing and most innovative of the developed countries. A growing body of research on economic development argues that these two facts are related. Productivity has been growing more rapidly because of technology development.[105] And capital has been flowing freely into R&D, new ventures, and advanced technology development at least in part because investors have been confident in the rules of the game, in the information they have, and in the information they will be able to get in the future about the firms in which they are investing.[106]

But the technology-driven transformation that is taking place in the corporate sector and in the economy as a whole may, ironically, be undermining the very market transparency that has helped to foster the growth and innovation of the past two decades. As intangible sources of wealth—new ideas, information, management systems, and relationships—have grown in importance relative to hard assets, the formal reporting systems that have provided critical information to investors for decades are becoming less and less relevant and informative. These systems, designed to capture critical information about the financial health of hard asset–based firms and the flow of resources through them, simply do not tell investors what they need to know about the true sources of wealth in today's economy.

Although capital had been still flowing to new ventures in general, and to the high-tech sector more specifically, the signs of underlying problems have become clearly evident. Quite a bit of air has come out of the dot-com bubble of 1999–2000, and prices of nearly all securities have become much more volatile on a day-to-day and week-to-week basis.[107] This market volatility inevitably makes investors more cautious and raises the cost of capital for new firms. Moreover, the lack of good information about the most important value drivers in individual firms, and in the economy as a whole, makes it more difficult for managers in firms and individual investors in the capital markets to make sensible resource allocation decisions. It also undermines the quality of measures of aggregate national economic performance, and therefore misleads policymakers, investors, and corporate strategic planners. It may consequently be producing a serious misallocation of society's resources that could be corrected with better information. Finally, to the extent that investors begin to suspect that insiders are selectively revealing important information, the valuable perception that the U.S. financial markets are fair will be undermined, making investors even more cautious and further raising the cost of capital.

While some uncertainty in the markets will always be unavoidable, the task force believes that much more can be done to improve the quality and informativeness of data assembled and reported by corporations to their investors, and of the data collected by statistical agencies to construct the national accounts. But we believe the problem will not be solved by private individuals acting under market pressures alone. Instead, a comprehensive multipronged effort must be undertaken at the federal level to reform financial reporting rules and to assemble the new data sources that the private sector needs to construct reliable and sensible new business models, better reflecting the dynamics of wealth creation in the twenty-first century. And we believe that increasing the certainty of intellectual property rights protection would assist this effort. We hope that our proposals will kick-start a badly needed national dialogue on these issues.

# The Brookings Task Force on Intangibles

T he Brookings Project on Intangibles grew out of a series of meetings in the late 1990s among a rather ad hoc group of individuals concerned about the changing role of intangibles in the economy and the public policy implications of these changes. In the fall of 1998, a task force was formed to examine systematically the policy issues raised by the growing importance of intangibles. In particular, the task force set out to identify problem areas in existing laws, regulations, and reporting requirements, as well as contexts in which government might play a positive role, and to recommend policy changes.

Margaret Blair and Steven M. H. Wallman served as co-chairs of the task force. Harold Kahn served as a senior adviser and arranged for the staff support provided by PricewaterhouseCoopers; Kristen Urban, Andrew Cantos, and Matthew Wissell served sequentially as recording secretary and staff assistant to the project. (A full list of task force members and their affiliations is provided at the end of this appendix.)

So as to best address all the relevant policy areas, the task force was organized into seven subgroups: Human Capital, Intellectual Property Rights, Strategic and Organizational Issues, Research and Development, Capital Market

Dimensions, SEC and Financial Reporting, and Tax Policy. This division of labor was intended to give the task force at least two perspectives on every issue that we thought might arise. The first four groups took the perspective of developers and users of different types of intangible inputs into production—intellectual property, human capital, organizational capital, and R&D—and were charged with looking at public policy issues as they affect a particular type of intangible. The last four groups (R&D is counted twice; see below) were each charged with looking at a particular policy area to see whether there are regulations, reporting requirements, or rules that might have adverse implications for investments in intangibles and to identify policy initiatives and changes that might lead to improvements in measuring and accounting for intangibles. The R&D subgroup had a dual role, looking both at government R&D policies, to consider how they influence behavior and choices in the private sector, and at R&D policies at the firm level, to see how those policies might be affected by a variety of government policies. Each subgroup recruited individuals to ensure that it had access to the full range of expertise necessary to address its given task.

The chair of each subgroup chose an appropriate methodology for collecting information and developing policy recommendations. For example, the Strategic and Organizational Issues subgroup, the SEC and Financial Reporting subgroup, and the Capital Markets Dimensions subgroup each conducted a series of extended interviews with appropriate experts, both within regulatory agencies and within firms. The R&D subgroup similarly brought in a number of industry experts to speak about issues of concern to them. Thus the reports of these subgroups not only drew on expertise within the subgroup but also took account of the perspective of a number of key outside experts. The other subgroups drew mainly on academic research and the expertise of their own members. After the subgroup chairs had drafted their reports, they met several times to hammer out agreement on which of their findings and recommendations should go into the task force report (the reports of each subgroup are available online at www.brookings.edu/es/research/projects/intangibles/intangibles.htm). In this way, questions that cut across the issues considered by specific subgroups were resolved among the subgroup chairs. Although subgroups did not meet to deliberate on the reports and recommendations of other subgroups, all members were given the opportunity to critique preliminary drafts of the task force report before deciding whether to endorse the final report.

### Task Force Members

*Project cochairs*

**Margaret M. Blair,** research director, Sloan-GULC Project on Business Institutions and Sloan Visiting Professor, Georgetown University Law Center; nonresident senior fellow, Brookings Institution

**Steven M. H. Wallman,** founder and chief executive officer, FOLIOfn; former commissioner, Securities and Exchange Commission

*Senior adviser*

**Harold Kahn,** chief financial officer, ScudderKemper Investments; former partner, PricewaterhouseCoopers

*Capital Market Dimensions subgroup*

**William W. Sihler (chair),** professor, Darden Graduate Business School

**Richard Crawford,** president, New Vision Financial

**P. Brett Hammond,** director of corporate projects, TIAA-CREF

**Robert E. Litan,** vice president and director, Economic Studies Program, Brookings Institution

*Human Capital subgroup*

**Laurie J. Bassi (chair),** director, research, Saba Software

**Ulf Johanson,** professor, School of Business, Stockholm University; president, Institute for Personnel and Corporate Development, Uppsala University

**Lisa M. Lynch,** William L. Clayton Professor of International Economic Affairs, Fletcher School of Law and Diplomacy, Tufts University

**Mark Mazzie,** chief knowledge officer, Morgan Stanley Dean Witter

**Daniel McMurrer,** research manager, Saba Software

**Marlene A. O'Connor,** professor, Stetson University College of Law

**Gregory Wurzburg,** principal administrator, Directorate for Education, Employment, Labor, and Social Affairs, Organization for Economic Cooperation and Development

*Intellectual Property subgroup*

**Gary Hoffman (chair),** partner, Dickstein Shapiro Morin & Oshinsky

**Jay Chatzkel,** principal, Progressive Practices

**David Johnson,** partner, Wilmer Cutler & Pickering

**Willy Manfroy Jr.,** principal, Bornival

**Francis Narin,** president, CHI Research

**Joseph M. Potenza,** partner, Banner & Witcoff

**Salvatore P. Tamburo,** associate, Dickstein Shapiro Morin & Oshinsky

*Research and Development Policy subgroup*

**Clark Eustace (chair),** honorary fellow, City University
Business School; formerly partner, Price Waterhouse

**Kent Hughes,** public policy scholar, Woodrow Wilson
Center

**Baruch Lev,** Philip Bardes Professor of Accounting and
Finance and director of the Vincent C. Ross Institute
of Accounting Research, New York University

**Stephen A. Merrill,** director of science, technology, and
economic policy, National Research Council

**Mark B. Myers,** senior vice president, research, Xerox
Corporation

**Sharon Oriel,** director, Global Intellectual Asset and
Capital Tech Center, Dow Chemical Company

*SEC and Financial Reporting subgroup*

**Jerry Arnold (chair),** professor of accounting, Leventhal
School of Accounting, University of Southern
California

**James F. Harrington,** partner, PricewaterhouseCoopers

**Earl Keller,** professor, College of Business, California
Polytechnic State University

**Alfred King,** chairman, Valuation Research Corporation

**Kurt Ramin,** International Accounting Standards
Committee

**Paul Zarowin,** professor, Department of Accounting,
Stern School of Business, New York University

*Strategic Organizational Issues subgroup*

**Jonathan Low (cochair),** senior fellow, Cap Gemini Ernst
& Young Center for Business Innovation

**Tony Siesfeld (cochair),** vice president, Mercer
Management Consulting

**Verna Allee,** president, Verna Allee Integral Performance Group

**Drew Bartkiewicz,** vice president, marketing, Broadvision.com

**Wendi R. Bukowitz,** consultant, PricewaterhouseCoopers

**Paul Osterman,** professor of human resources and management, Massachusetts Institute of Technology

**Lawrence Prusak,** executive director, IBM Institute of Knowledge Management

*Tax Policy subgroup*

**Andrew Lyon (chair),** professor, Economics Department, University of Maryland

**George Mundstock,** professor, School of Law, University of Miami

**Melbert Schwarz,** director, legislative and regulatory services, Washington National Tax, KPMG

*Project Staff Support*

**Kristen Urban,** (then) principal consultant, PricewaterhouseCoopers

**Andrew Cantos,** principal consultant, PricewaterhouseCoopers

**Matthew Wissell,** senior manager, PricewaterhouseCoopers

*Bibliographic assistance*

**Lee Bloomquist,** senior researcher, Steelcase

# Notes

1. Microsoft Corp., "Microsoft_2000," annual report (www.microsoft.com/msft/ar00/balance.htm [January 2001]). Market capitalization is based on market value of equity (5.283 billion shares outstanding, at $60 per share) plus $10.8 billion in liabilities.

2. See S. L. Mintz, "Seeing Is Believing: A Better Approach to Estimating Knowledge Capital," *CFO*, February 1999, pp. 29–37, discussing "knowledge capital" measurement methodology developed by Professor Baruch Lev of New York University. Mintz estimates that as of May 31, 1998, Merck had more than $48 billion in knowledge capital, and Pfizer had nearly $24 billion.

3. See, for example, "Retail Link Is on the Cutting Edge," *Business and Industry*, vol. 15 (May 1998), p. 70, for a discussion of the software used to manage Walmart's so-called vendor managed inventory system.

4. For an example involving Ford Motor Co., see Keith Bradsher, "Can Motor City Come up with a Clean Machine?" *New York Times*, May 19, 1999, p. C1. Image may also be a critical factor for Microsoft in its court battle with the antitrust authorities.

5. Charles Goldfinger, "Intangible Economy and Its Implication for Statistics and Statisticians," *International Statistical Review*, vol. 65 (August 1997), pp. 191–220, citing Conseil Economique et Social (CES), "Les Leviers Immateriels de l'Action Economique" (Paris, May 1994).

6. See Barry P. Bosworth and Jack E. Triplett, "Numbers Matter," Policy Brief 63 (Brookings, July 2000), for a discussion of the problems of measuring productivity in the service sector.

7. One of the task force co-chairs took an early lead in addressing these issues. See Steven M. H. Wallman, "The Future of Accounting and Disclosure in an Evolving World: The Need for Dramatic Change," *Accounting Horizons*, vol. 9 (September 1995), pp. 103–16.

8. Leandro Canibano and Paloma Sanchez, "Measuring Intangibles to Understand and Improve Innovation Management," research proposal, Universidad Autonoma, Madrid, 1998, note that the adjective *intangible* can accompany various concepts, such as assets, investments, resources, or other phenomena. The transformation of the adjective into a noun is suggestive of the absence of a broadly accepted definition. Numerous definitions and classifications have been proposed, particularly during the past decade. See also Ulf Johanson and others, "Human Resource Costing and Accounting versus the Balanced Scorecard: A Literature Survey of Experience with the Concepts," working paper (Stockholm University School of Business, 1999). Some analysts have limited the definition of intangibles to those factors over which legal rights have been clearly assigned, such as patents, copyrights, and brands. See Baruch Lev, *Intangibles: Management, Measurement, and Reporting* (Brookings, 2001); Leonard Nakamura, "Intangibles: What Put the *New* in the New Economy?" Federal Reserve Bank of Philadelphia *Business Review* (July–August 1999), pp. 3–16. We use a broader definition in order to include factors such as organizational features, individual knowledge and skills, or networks of business relationships, over which property rights may not be well defined.

9. Cited in Nakamura, "Intangibles," p. 11.

10. Bureau of Economic Analysis, National Income and Product Accounts, table 1.1 (www.bea.doc.gov/bea/dn1.htm [January 2001]).

11. Robert E. Hall, "The Stock Market and Capital Accumulation," Working Paper 7180 (Cambridge, Mass.: National Bureau of Economic Research, June 1999), quote is from p. 4; Robert E. Hall, "E-Capital: The Link between the Stock Market and the Labor Market in the 1990s," *Brookings Papers on Eco-*

*nomic Activity,* 2:2000, pp. 73–118. Lev, *Intangibles,* finds that for firms in the S&P 500 index, the average ratio of market value of equity to net book value had risen from a little over 1 in the late 1970s to more than 6 by the late 1990s. Hall, using a conceptually similar but methodologically different approach, finds that the ratio of the market value of all financial claims (debt plus equity) on corporations to the reproduction cost of property, plant, and equipment had risen from around 0.8 in the mid-1970s to nearly 1.8 in the mid-1990s. By the end of 1999, the ratio exceeded 2. Hall's findings suggest that the current high levels of this ratio are similar to or slightly above levels reached in the mid-1960s, but by Lev's measure the current levels are unprecedented.

12. Authors' calculations based on the 1999 annual reports of Walt Disney Co. (disney.go.com/investors/annual99/dis99ar55.html [January 2001]) and Sprint Corp. (ww3.sprint.com/sprint/annual/99/delivering/shareholders/shareholders.html [January 2001]) and stock price quotations from the *Wall Street Journal,* August 3, 2000. The extraordinary volatility and dramatic movements in equity prices in the second half of 2000, especially in the Internet stock sector, demonstrate the need for far greater transparency in understanding the drivers of wealth production, especially in the high-tech and knowledge-based industries. Otherwise, as we argue below, one can expect to see continued high volatility as the markets attempt to calibrate values with too little information.

13. Bronwyn H. Hall, "Innovation and Market Value," in Ray Barrell, Geoffrey Mason, and Mary O'Mahoney, eds., *Productivity, Innovation and Economic Performance* (Cambridge University Press, 2000), finds that the market value of the modern manufacturing corporation is strongly related to its knowledge assets.

14. Erik Brynjolfsson and Shinkyu Yang, "The Intangible Costs and Benefits of Computer Investments: Evidence from Financial Markets" (Sloan School of Management, Massachusetts Institute of Technology, April 1999); Hall, "The Stock Market and Capital Accumulation," p. 28.

15. See Timothy F. Bresnahan, Erik Brynjolfsson, and Lorin M. Hitt, "Technology, Organization, and the Demand for Skilled

Labor," in Margaret M. Blair and Thomas A. Kochan, eds., *The New Relationship: Human Capital in the American Corporation* (Brookings, 2000), pp. 175–78.

16. In 1996 the average ratio of R&D spending to sales of electronics, drugs, software, and biotech companies were, respectively, 6.1 percent, 12 percent, 17.8 percent, and 41 percent, compared with an overall average for manufacturing of around 4 percent; see Baruch Lev, "R&D and Capital Markets," *Bank of America Journal of Applied Corporate Finance*, vol. 11 (Winter 1999), pp. 21–35. On the link between R&D spending and market-to-book ratios, see Hall, "Innovation and Market Value"; Baruch Lev and Theodore Sougiannis, "Penetrating the Book-to-Market Black Box: The R&D Effect," *Journal of Business Finance and Accounting*, vol. 26 (April–May 1999); Bronwyn Hall, Adam Jaffe, and Manual Trajtenberg, "Market Value and Patent Citations: A First Look," Working Paper 7741 (Cambridge, Mass.: National Bureau of Economic Research, 2000); Brynjolfsson and Yang, "The Intangible Costs and Benefits of Computer Investments." Louis K. C. Chan, Josef Lakonishok, and Theodore Sougiannis, "The Stock Market Valuation of Research and Development Expenditures," working paper (University of Illinois at Urbana-Champaign, June 1999) find that stocks of R&D-intensive firms tend to outperform stocks of firms with little or no R&D, but they interpret this to mean that the market fails to give such firms sufficient credit for the value of their R&D investments.

17. See Sandra A. Black and Lisa M. Lynch, "Human-Capital Investments and Productivity," *American Economic Review*, vol. 86, no. 2 (1996), pp. 263–67; Laurie J. Bassi and others, "Profiting from Learning: Do Firms' Investments in Education and Training Pay Off?" white paper (Alexandria, Va.: American Society for Training and Development, September 2000).

18. Carolyn Kay Brancato, "New Corporate Performance Measures," Report 1118-95-RR (New York: Conference Board, 1995), quotes are from p. 9; Carolyn Kay Brancato, "Communicating Corporate Performance: A Delicate Balance," Special Report 97-1 (New York: Conference Board, 1997).

19. Cap Gemini Ernst & Young's Center for Business Innovation has sponsored several major research reports in the last few

years on the correlation between intangibles and market value or financial results; see, for example, *Measures that Matter* (Cambridge, Mass., March 1997); *Managing the Success of the IPO Transformation Process* (Cambridge, Mass., June 1998); *The Value Creation Index* (Cambridge, Mass., June 2000). It also co-published a book with the Organization for Economic Cooperation and Development (OECD) entitled *Enterprise Value in the Knowledge Economy: Measuring Performance in the Age of Intangibles* (Cambridge, Mass.: Center for Business and Innovation, December 1997). PricewaterhouseCoopers has developed a new business reporting model called "ValueReporting"; see Robert Eccles and others, *The ValueReporting Revolution: Moving Beyond the Earnings Game* (Wiley, 2001). And in August 2000, Arthur Andersen gave a $10 million grant to the Massachusetts Institute of Technology's Sloan School of Management to develop a "New Economy Value Research Lab." See Steffan Heuer, "The Bean Counters Strike Back," *The Standard*, August 21, 2000.

20. See Jeffrey Arthur, "Effects of Human Resource Systems on Manufacturing Performance and Turnover," *Academy of Management Journal*, vol. 37 (June 1994), pp. 670–87; Laurie Bassi and Mark VanBuren, "Valuing Investments in Intellectual Capital," *International Journal of Technology Management*, vol. 18, nos. 5, 6, 7, 8 (1999), pp. 414–32; Brian E. Becker and Mark A. Huselid, "High Performance Work Systems and Firm Performance: A Synthesis of Research and Managerial Applications," *Research in Personnel and Human Resources* (forthcoming); Marvin L. Bouillon, B. Michael Doran, and Peter F. Orazem, "Human Capital Investment Effects on Firm Returns," *Journal of Applied Business Research,*vol. 12 (Winter 1995); Huselid, "The Impact of Human Resource Management Practices on Turnover, Productivity, and Corporate Financial Performance," *Academy of Management Journal*, vol. 38, no. 3 (1995), pp. 635–72; and Casey Ichniowski and Kathryn Shaw, "The Impact of HRM Practices on Performance: An International Perspective," working paper (Department of Labor, December 1996).

21. A study by Burson-Marsteller, a public relations firm, found that CEO reputation has a significant impact on the overall reputation of a firm. In a survey of 1,400 corporate stakeholders

in 1999, the company found that 88 percent said they would buy stock on the basis of the CEO's reputation, 87 percent said they would recommend a company as a good joint venture partner on that basis, 81 percent said they would believe in a company under media pressure on that basis, and 80 percent said they would recommend a company as a good place to work on that basis. See Burson-Marsteller, "Maximizing CEO Reputation" (www.ceogo. com/research/research011.html [January 2001]).

22. See Laurie J. Bassi and others, "Measuring Corporate Investments in Human Capital," in Margaret M. Blair and Thomas A Kochan, eds., *The New Relationship: Human Capital in the American Corporation* (Brookings, 2000).

23. See Financial Accounting Standards Board, "Elements of Financial Statements," Statement of Financial Accounting Concepts 6 (December 1985).

24. For purposes of the national accounts, statisticians at the Department of Commerce have also begun recognizing "software" as a separate asset category.

25. In corporate accounting, special rules and categories are applicable in certain industries. In the oil industry, for example, oil companies may choose between "successful efforts" and "full cost" accounting approaches when recording expenditures associated with searching for oil and gas. If oil or gas is found, the search costs associated with a particular discovery may be capitalized ("successful efforts"), while all other exploration costs are immediately expensed. Alternatively, companies may choose to expense all exploration costs immediately. Similarly, film production companies are permitted to "capitalize" some of the costs of making a film for book accounting purposes, and then take a depreciation charge in each subsequent year over the expected commercial life of the property. And some accountants have begun recognizing "in-process R&D" as a separate category of assets in accounting for corporate acquistions.

26. See Jorgen Mortensen, Clark Eustace, and Karel Lannoo, "Intangibles in the European Economy" (Brussels: Center for European Policy Studies, March 1997), p. 22.

27. A recent study commissioned by the European Commission examined changes underway in the approach to R&D inside firms. See "The Intangible Economy: Impact and Policy

Issues," Report of the European High Level Expert Group on the Intangible Economy (Brussels: European Commission, 2000), pp. 8–10.

28. In the summer of 2000, a small company called Emulex saw its stock price collapse from $103 per share to $45 per share in fifteen minutes when Bloomberg News posted a press release saying that the firm's chief executive had resigned, net earnings would be restated, and the SEC had begun an investigation into its accounting practices. The price recovered quickly once it was widely published that this information was not true. See Alex Berenson, "On Hair-Trigger Wall Street, A Stock Plunges on False News," *New York Times,* August 26, 2000, p. A1. See also Charles J. Fombrun, *Reputation: Realizing Value from the Corporate Image* (Harvard Business School Press, 1996).

29. One of the earliest known examples of ABS financing was a $100 million bond issue by Dow Chemicals in 1994, backed by its patent portfolio. In 1999, Formula 1 issued a $1.4 billion bond backed by its intellectual property rights in contracts covering event staging and performance rights and media, broadcast, and advertising rights. For more details, see Clark Eustace, "Intellectual Property and the Capital Markets," working paper (London: City University Business School, May 2000), appendix 4.

30. However, see also Ronald J. Mann, "Secured Credit and Software Financing," Law and Economics Working Paper 99-014 (University of Michigan, 1999), on the difficulties of using software as collateral for debt finance.

31. See Eustace, "Intellectual Property and the Capital Markets," p. 10.

32. See Hall, "Innovation and Market Value"; Lev and Sougiannis, "Penetrating the Book-to-Market Black Box"; Hall, Jaffe and Trajtenberg, "Market Value and Patent Citations"; and Brynjolfsson and Yang, "The Intangible Costs and Benefits of Computer Investments."

33. Examples include the "balanced scorecard" developed by Robert Norton and David Kaplan (David P. Kaplan and Robert S. Norton, "Putting the Balanced Scorecard to Work," *Harvard Business Review* [September–October 1993]); the "dashboard" model developed by the Conference Board (Bran-

cato, "Communicating Corporate Performance"); the "Navigator" model developed by Skandia Corp. (Skandia Corp., "Intellectual Capital Report," supplement to *Annual Financial Report* [Stockholm: various years] and Leif Edvinsson and Michael Malone, *Intellectual Capital* [Harpers, 1997]); the ValueReporting model developed by PricewaterhouseCoopers (Pricewaterhouse-Coopers, *ValueReporting Forecast 2000* [2000]); the "employee-customer profit chain" model developed at Sears, Roebuck (see J. Anthony Rucci, Steven P. Kirk, and Richard T. Quinn, "The Employee-Customer Profit Chain at Sears," *Harvard Business Review* [January–February, 1998]); and the annual *Report to Society* developed by Shell UK as a mechanism for tracking and disclosing nonfinancial performance information.

34. See the report of the task force's Strategic Organizational Issues subgroup (www.brookings.edu/es/research/projects/intangibles/intangibles.htm).

35. See Bosworth and Triplett, "Numbers Matter," for a discussion of the policy problems that result from faulty data on productivity in the service sector. The federal agencies responsible for compiling macroeconomic performance statistics are well aware of the measurement problems arising from poor information about intangibles and other aspects of the New Economy. See Economics and Statistics Administration, *Digital Economy 2000* (Department of Commerce, June 2000).

36. See Nakamura, "Intangibles." Nakamura's research predated most of the truly egregious run-up in the stock prices of "dot.com" companies in the second half of 1999. Many of these companies had no profits and would not have had profits even if their R&D expenditures had been capitalized. But as of this writing, stock prices in the dot.com sector have undergone a substantial correction. If financial markets had access to better information about the intangible assets in these companies, prices might never have become so volatile in the first place.

37. See Chan, Lakonishok, and Sougiannis, "The Stock Market Valuation of Research and Development Expenditures."

38. Lev, *Intangibles.*

39. See Securities and Exchange Commission, "Selective Disclosure and Insider Trading," Release 33-7881, August 15,

2000 (www.sec.gov/rules/final/33-7881.htm). The rule took effect on October 23, 2000.

40. See, for example, Scott Thurm, "Mum's the Word in the Wake of Disclosure Rule," *Wall Street Journal*, August 16, 2000, p. C1.

41. Such information would have to be standardized—with well-defined terms and consistent approaches to measurement—and susceptible to audit or verification, or such enhanced disclosure could quickly deteriorate into a safe harbor for extravagant, and even fraudulent, claims. The task force is sensitive to this issue and recognizes that it will not be easy or costless to develop reporting standards for intangibles (see the discussion below). Our intent here is to call attention to the swelling costs of not having good information.

42. Quoted in Brancato, "Communicating Corporate Performance," p. 12.

43. Shell UK's annual *Report to Society* is published at least in part because of the company's awareness that, given the sometimes messy nature of its resource extraction and processing work, it is a conspicuous target for environmental activists. Also, many of the company's operations are in developing countries, where it must sometimes make deals with political leaders who do not necessarily share developed country values about democracy or business ethics. See "Multinationals and Their Morals," *Economist*, December 2, 1995, p. 18. The company concedes its vulnerability in these areas in its 1998 report: "we accept that we still have some way to go before we can clearly demonstrate that environmental and social factors are automatically built into our business strategy and individual decision-making processes, or that these factors balance the financial bottom line except in extreme circumstances. So, how do we as a company ensure that sustainable development issues are not forgotten? What are we doing to ensure that sustainable development informs and guides 'bottom line' business decisions?" *Shell UK Report to Society*, (London, 1998), p. 28.

44. Rucci, Kirk, and Quinn, "The Employee-Customer Profit Chain at Sears."

45. See the report of the task force's SEC and Financial Reporting subgroup (www.brookings.edu/es/research/projects/

intangibles/intangibles.htm). Members of this subgroup met in 1999 with representatives of the Financial Executives Institute's Committee on Corporate Reporting (preparers); the Financial Accounting Policy Committee of the Association for Investment Management and Research (investors and users); the American Institute of Certified Public Accountants Auditing Standards Board (auditors); the Financial Accounting Standards Board (standard setters); and the Securities and Exchange Commission (regulators).

46. One of the professionals interviewed by the SEC and Financial Reporting subgroup called the problem of reporting on intangibles "a pretty complex, judgmental thing to do," and another interviewee noted that "there would be a lot of practical difficulties in trying to measure and track intangibles in particularly soft areas." A third noted that the value of many intangibles is "so intertwined with all the other elements" that attempting to identify and report separate values for separate elements might "add more distortion to the reporting as opposed to less distortion." (Interview notes of subgroup chair, Jerry Arnold.)

47. See Financial Accounting Standards Board, "Qualitative Characteristics of Accounting Information," Statements of Financial Accounting Concepts 2 (May 1980), paras. 91–93.

48. See Brancato, "Communicating Corporate Performance," p. 7.

49. See Leslie Kaufman, "Cutting through the Fog of Growth for Net Retailers," *New York Times*, September 1, 1999, p. B1. Beginning in the fourth quarter of 1999, however, under pres-sure from analysts to provide more relevant information, Amazon.com began releasing quarterly and annual data on sales per "active" customer, which it defined as any customer who had bought something in the previous twelve months. See "Amazon.com Announces Profitability in U.S.-based Book Sales, Financial Results for Fourth Quarter, 1999," press release, February 2, 2000.

50. Section 11 of the Securities Act makes corporate directors, officers, and other agents personally liable for misstatements in securities registration documents. SEC Rule 10b-5, promulgated pursuant to section 10(b) of the Securities Exchange Act of 1934, makes it unlawful for corporations or their agents, "in

connection with the purchase or sale of any security," to "make any untrue statement of a material fact or to omit to state a material fact necessary in order to make the statements made, in light of the circumstances under which they were made, not misleading." This rule has been interpreted broadly by the courts to cover press releases and other more casual statements by corporate officers to investors who are trading in the firm's stock in the secondary market, even if neither the firm itself nor any of its officers or directors is either buying or selling its own securities at the time of the statement. See, for example, *Basic Inc.* v. *Levinson,* 485 U.S. 224, 108 S.Ct. 978.

51. 15 U.S.C. secs. 77a et seq. (1994 and Supp. 1, 1995). The 1995 law protects companies from liability for forward-looking statements if those statements also include cautionary language identifying factors that could change the outcome. See Marc I. Steinberg, "Symposium: Securities Law after the Private Securities Litigation Reform Act—Unfinished Business," *SMU Law Review*, vol. 50, no. 9 (1996). Early reports claimed that companies did not increase the quantity or quality of forward-looking information that they provided as a result of the act, but they did use more cautionary language in public documents. See Patrice Duggan Samuals, "Investing It: Litigation Law Creates Work for Disclaimer Writers," *New York Times*, April 14, 1996, sec. 3, p. 3. But see also Marilyn F. Johnson, Ron Kasnik, and Karen Nelson, "The Impact of Securities Litigation Reform on the Disclosure of Forward-Looking Information by High-Technology Firms," *Journal of Accounting Research* (forthcoming), which finds that firms in the computer (hardware and software) and pharmaceuticals industries have been much more likely to report forward-looking information since the passage of this act, and that the safe harbor has had no adverse impact on the quality of forward-looking information released by management.

52. Financial Accounting Standards Board, "Business Combinations and Intangible Assets," September 7, 1999. This proposed rule change sparked enormous controversy and resistance in the business community, as discussed below. In December 2000, the FASB modified its proposal to allow U.S. companies to continue making acquisitions without having to take large periodic earnings write-downs. See Jonathan Weil, "FASB Backs

Down on Goodwill-Accounting Rules," *Wall Street Journal,* December 7, 2000, p. A2.

53. See Albert B.Crenshaw, "A Tech Push to Keep 'Pooling' on Books," *Washington Post,* June 25, 2000, p. H1.

54. Patrick E. Hopkins, Richard W. Houston, and Michael F. Peters, "Purchase, Pooling, and Equity Analysts' Valuation Judgments," *Accounting Review,* vol. 75 (July 2000), find evidence that financial analysts' stock-price judgments are lowest when a company applies the purchase method of accounting for a merger and ratably amortizes the acquisition premium.

55. See, for example, Elizabeth Demers and Baruch Lev, "A Rude Awakening: Internet Shakeout in 2000," working paper (University of Rochester, 2000), noting that factors that appear to be important in the valuation of dot-com companies in one year may bear no relation to value the next year.

56. Lev, *Intangibles.*

57. See Kevin A. Hassett, "Outlaw Selective Disclosure? No, the More Information, the Better," *Wall Street Journal*, Aug. 10, 2000, p. A18.

58. U.S. Constitution, art. 1, sec. 8, cl. 8.

59. See Donald A. Gregory, Charles W. Saber, and Jon D. Grossman, *Introduction to Intellectual Property Law* (Washington: Bureau of National Affairs, 1994), p. 7.

60. Gregory, Saber, and Grossman, *Introduction to Intellectual Property Law,* p. 1.

61. The importance of copyright law in determining who is able to capture the economic value of artistic works was dramatized in summer 2000 in the legal fight over the operations of Napster, Inc. Based in Redwood City, Calif., the company operated a website that allowed users to share electronic copies of songs and other music recordings with each other. Napster attracted 23 million customers within a few months, but in late July the U.S. District Court in San Francisco ruled that the company's operations violated the legal protection of the artists and record companies who held copyrights to the music being exchanged through the service. See Matt Richtel, "In Victory for Recording Industry, Judge Bars Online Music Sharing," *New York Times,* July 27, 2000, p. A1. In late February, a federal appeals court upheld the lower court ruling. See David Streitfeld

and Christopher Stern, "Napster Must Halt Online Music Swaps," *Washington Post*, February 13, 2001, p. A1.

62. National Science Foundation, *Science and Engineering Indicators 2000,* app. tab. 2-3 (www.nsf.gov/sbe/srs/seind00/start. htm). In the late 1980s, at the height of the Reagan era military build-up, the federal government funded around 30 percent of R&D carried out by industry.

63. For information on the Malcolm Baldrige National Quality Award program, see NIST's website (www.nist.gov).

64. Securities Act of 1933, sec. 19(a); Securities Exchange Act of 1934, sec. 13(b)(1). See also Securities and Exchange Commission, "Statement of Policy on the Establishment and Improvement of Accounting Principles and Standards," *Codification of Financial Reporting Policies,* sec. 101. The professional organizations authorized by the SEC to develop the accounting principles were the Committee on Accounting Procedures, 1939–59; the Accounting Principles Board, 1959–73; and since 1973 the Financial Accounting Standards Board.

65. "Spillovers occur when one company's innovation—say, the development of an improved memory computer chip—stimulates a flood of related innovations and technical improvements by other companies and industries." Andrew B. Abel and Ben S. Bernanke, *Macroeconomics*, 3d ed. (Addison-Wesley, 1998), p. 212. See also Edward N. Wolff and Nadiri M. Ishaq, "Spillover Effects, Linkage Structure and Research and Development," in *Structural Change and Economic Dynamics,* vol. 4 (December 1993), pp. 315–31.

66. See the report of the task force's Strategic Organizational Issues subgroup.

67. Appointed to the post in 1991, Edvinsson is believed to have been the first "vice president for intellectual capital" at any company in the world. He is currently visiting professor in knowledge economics and intellectual capital at the University of Lund, Sweden, and president of Universal Networking Intellectual Capital.

68. Quoted in Brancato, "Communicating Corporate Performance," pp. 68–69.

69. For a related, but more detailed, parsing of the measurement problem, see Steven M. H. Wallman, "The Future of Accounting and Financial Reporting, Part II: The Colorized

Approach," *Accounting Horizons*, vol. 10 (June 1996), pp. 138–48.

70. The accounting treatment of certain kinds of liabilities, such as maintenance, servicing, and environmental liabilities, and risk-hedging and financial instruments and derivatives, present similar problems.

71. There is evidence that outside investors do care about employment and personnel policies. Institutional Shareholder Services, a division of Thompson International that advises large institutional investors on proxy matters, recently endorsed an employee-led shareholder proposal at IBM urging that the company permit employees to choose whether to remain in a traditional pension plan or switch to a new cash-balance plan. IBM had initially announced that all employees would be required to switch to the new plan except those within five years of retirement, but under pressure from unhappy employees and negative publicity, it agreed to allow all workers age forty and older and with at least ten years of service to choose between the plans. See Jon G. Auerbach and Ellen E. Schultz, "Shareholder-Services Group Supports Workers Choice on IBM Pension Plan," *Wall Street Journal,* April 17, 2000, p. B6. To the extent that employees can be required or induced to switch to the cash-balance plans, IBM would probably be able to record higher current profits. Although many institutional investors apparently decided that the negative effect on employee morale would cost the firm more in the long run, other shareholders did not agree. The resolution won only 28.4 percent of the vote, and therefore was defeated. See Ellen E. Schultz and John G. Auerbach, "IBM Holders Defeat Pension Resolution," *Wall Street Journal*, April 26, 2000, p. A2.

72. See Robert E. Litan and Peter J. Wallison, *The GAAP Gap: Corporate Disclosure in the Age of the Internet* (Washington: American Enterprise Institute—Brookings Joint Center on Regulatory Studies, forthcoming).

73. Three task force subgroups proposed some sort of public-private data collection effort. For details, see reports of the Human Capital, the Strategic Organizational Issues, and the R&D Policy subgroups (www.brookings/org/es/research/projects/intangibles.htm).

74. In recent months, a number of leaders in the accounting profession have expressed interest in the potential of a new com-

puter language, eXtensible Markup Language (XML), to greatly reduce the cost of capturing all kinds of data and making them available to multiple users over the Internet. See, for example, Mike Willis, "Corporate Communications for the 21st Century," white paper (New York: PricewaterhouseCoopers, 2000). The American Institute of Certified Public Accountants has embarked on a project to develop eXtensible Business Reporting Language (XBRL), based on XML, which can be used to speed up the publication of financial information on the Internet. See Litan and Wallison, *The GAAP Gap,* chap. 4, for a discussion of this initiative. For detailed information on XML see (www.xml.org), and on XBRL, see (www.xbrl.org).

75. See Organization for Economic Cooperation and Development, "Main Definitions and Conventions for the Measurement of Research and Experimental Development (R&D): A Summary of the Frascati Manual 1993," OECD/GD(94)84 (Paris, 1994).

76. Chartered Institute of Management Accountants, "Accounting for R&D" (London, 1992).

77. See Shelley Taylor and Associates, *Full Disclosure 2000: An International Study of Disclosure Practices* (London, October 2000), for detailed tabulation of the disclosure practices of one hundred large international and domestic corporations.

78. See, for example, the "Intangible Assets Monitor" published as part of Swedish consulting firm Celemi's annual report; Skandia Corp., *Human Capital in Transformation: Intellectual Capital Prototype Report* (Stockholm, 1998); Royal-Dutch/Shell, *Shell in the UK Report to Society 2000*; and Ford Motor Co.'s *Connecting with Society: 1999 Corporate Citizenship Report* (Michigan: University Lithoprinters, 1999).

79. The Danish Ministry of Business has issued a series of reports detailing an initiative to develop a framework for reporting on intellectual capital. See Danish Trade and Industry Development Council, "Intellectual Capital Accounts: Reporting and Managing Intellectual Capital" (Copenhagen, May 1997). The Organization for Economic Cooperation and Development, together with the Dutch Ministries of Economic Affairs and of Education, Culture, and Science, sponsored an international symposium on "Measuring and Reporting Intellectual Capital" in

June 1999. The symposium chairman's conclusions are available at (www.oecd.org/dsti/sti/industry/indcomp/act/ams-conf/conclusions.htm). See also the OECD's website on value creation (www.oecd.org/daf/corporate-affaris/disclosure/intangibles.htm). Under the auspices of the Meritum Project (Measuring Intangibles to Understand and Improve Innovation), sponsored by the European Commission, nine universities and research institutes in Denmark, Finland, France, Norway, Spain, and Sweden are investigating the feasibility of measuring and reporting on intangibles. Final reports of this project are to be filed with the commission in May 2001. The Global Reporting Initiative, a project of the Coalition for Environmentally Responsible Economies (CERES) is developing guidelines for reporting on the sustainability of companies' environmental policies. See CERES, "Sustainability Reporting Guidelines: Exposure Draft for Public Comment and Pilot Testing" (Toronto, 1999). See also Centre for Tomorrow's Company, "Sooner, Sharper, Simpler: A Lean Vision of an Inclusive Annual Report" (London, n.d.); Swedish Public Relations Association, "Report on Communications" (Stockholm, 1996), on a project to develop better information about the growing role of intangibles in the economy.

80. See, for example, Robert K. Elliott, chairman, American Institute of Certified Public Accountants, "Statement before the Senate Committee on Banking, Housing, and Urban Affairs, Subcommittee on Securities Concerning Financial Reporting Methods for the Twenty-First Century," July 19, 2000.

81. Cite to discussion of this issue in Lev, *Intangibles*. See also Steven J. Monahan, "Conservatism, Growth and the Role of Accounting Numbers in the Equity Valuation Process," working paper (University of Chicago, October 18, 1999), discussing empirical evidence on the information content of various accounting treatments for R&D. Under the current accounting model, once an item is classified as an asset on the balance sheet, its cost is systematically charged to expense over time through a depreciation charge during its useful life, rather than to current expenses. In theory, this will produce a better measure of the current use of the asset. But as evidence that this gradual allocation of the costs over time is not as useful to investors as some believe, many financial analysts use a statistic known as

EBITDA (earnings before interest, taxes, depreciation, and amortization)—in which depreciation, as well as interest and taxes, are added back to earnings—to get a measure of the current cash flows being generated by the firm.

82. See report of the task force's SEC and Financial Reporting subgroup.

83. In its so-called Jenkins Report, the AICPA recommends expanded segment disclosure. AICPA Special Committee on Financial Reporting, "Improving Business Reporting—A Customer Focus: Meeting the Information Needs of Investors and Creditors" (Jersey City, N.J., 1994).

84. See the report of the task force's SEC and Financial Reporting subgroup.

85. Ibid.

86. See, for example, Wallman, "The Future of Accounting and Financial Reporting, Part II"; Mark Clare and Arthur W. Detore, *Knowledge Assets: Professional's Guide to Valuation and Financial Management* (Harcourt Professional Publishing, 2000); PricewaterhouseCoopers, *ValueReporting Forecast: 2000*; David P. Kaplan and Robert S. Norton, "The Balanced Scorecard: Measures that Drive Performance," *Harvard Business Review* (January–February 1992), p. 71; and Kaplan and Norton, "Putting the Balanced Scorecard to Work."

87. See, for example, Steven M. H. Wallman, "The Future of Accounting and Financial Reporting, Part IV: 'Access' Accounting," *Accounting Horizons*, vol. 11 (June 1997), pp. 103–16, which outlines a "Direct Access Reporting Model."

88. Litan and Wallison, *The GAAP Gap,* suggest that even the raw data that go into the construction of financial and non-financial performance measures could and should be made available electronically to investors, analysts, and other interested parties. See also Bernard S. Black, "Information Asymmetry, the Internet, and Securities Offerings," Working Paper 139 (Columbia Law School, Center for Law and Economic Studies, May 1998), noting that "reputational intermediaries" would still be needed to attest to the quality and relevance of the raw information and of the protocols used to construct aggregates.

89. For further discussion, see the report of the task force's Intellectual Property subgroup (www.brookings.edu/es/research/projects/intangibles/intangibles.htm).

90. If the specialized patent court were based in a single location (say, Washington, D.C.), it might be prohibitively remote to some potential litigants. The idea of specialized trial courts for patent cases has been discussed by others; see, for example, Ernest Shriver, "Separate but Equal: Intellectual Property Importation and the Recent Amendments to Section 337," *Minnesota Journal of Global Trade,* vol. 5 (Summer 1996), p. 449; Gregory D. Leibold, "In Juries We Do not Trust: Appellate Review of Patent-Infringement Litigation," *University of Colorado Law Review,* vol. 67 (Summer 1996), p. 648. Some members of the task force suggested making use of specialized juries to hear patent cases, but there was no consensus on that idea.

91. Commerce Secretary William Daley has also expressed support for this idea. See "Daley Calls for Renewed Effort to Negotiate Global Patent System," *Patent, Trademark and Copyright Journal*, September 16, 1999, pp. 552–53.

92. 149 F.3d 1368 (Fed. Cir. 1998), cert. denied, 119 S.Ct. 851 (1999).

93. 172 F.3d 1352 (Fed. Cir. 1999).

94. See, for example, Claus D. Melarti, "*State Street Bank & Trust Co.* v. *Signature Financial Group, Inc.*: Ought the Mathematical Algorithm and Business Method Exceptions Return to Business as Usual?" *Journal of Intellectual Property Law,* vol. 6 (Spring 1999), pp. 387–89.

95. 15 U.S.C. secs. 1051 et seq.

96. WIPO is well aware that international trademark disputes will proliferate because of the global nature of the Internet while trademark law only protects competing marks in a common geographical area. See "Multimedia Developments of Note," *Multimedia and Web Strategist,* vol. 4 (August 1998).

97. See Ian Ballon and Keith M. Kupferschmid, "Intellectual Property Opportunities and Pitfalls in the Conduct of Electronic Commerce," *Practising Law Institute/Pat,* vol. 563 (June 1999), p. 103.

98. The recent controversies regarding the storing and sharing of music on the Internet, however, has raised new questions that may eventually require a reexamination of the strength of copyright protection in this area.

99. See Brenda Tiffany Dieck, "Reevaluating the Forum Non Conveniens Doctrine in Multilateral Copyright Cases," *Washington Law Review*, vol. 74 (January 1999), pp. 131–32.

100. To complicate matters further, there are other issues, too. Expenditures made by a company to acquire the intangible assets of a target corporation in a takeover are deductible over a fifteen-year period, but the expenditures made by the *target* company in the course of the same takeover may be treated as nondeductible capital expenditures.

101. See the report of the task force's Tax Policy subgroup at (www.brookings.edu/es/research/projects/intangibles/intangibles.htm).

102. As recently as 1997, however, a survey of intellectual property companies conducted for the Intellectual Property Institute by Mark Bezant and Richard Punt of the Arthur Andersen Economic and Financial Consulting Practice in London found that few had bothered to discuss with their lenders the possibility of using intangibles as collateral for loans. Those that had broached the subject reported that lenders were unwilling to consider the idea. Bezant and Punt also noted that when assessing the assets of a firm in liquidation, the credit-evaluating agency Standard and Poor's says that it places a smaller value on intangibles than on tangibles. Mark Bezant and Richard Punt, *The Use of Intellectual Property as Security for Debt Finance* (London: Intellectual Property Institute, 1998).

103. See the report of the task force's Capital Market Dimensions subgroup at (www.brookings.edu/es/research/projects/intangibles/intangibles.htm).

104. For more discussion of these issues, see the report of the task force's R&D Policy subgroup.

105. See Dale Jorgenson and Keven Stiroh, "Raising the Speed Limit: U.S. Economic Growth in the Information Age," *Brookings Papers on Economic Activity, 1:2000,* pp. 125–235.

106. From 1970 to 1996, investment in R&D, training, and advertising caught up with and overtook investment in tangibles in the U.S. economy. See Eustace, "Intellectual Property and the Capital Markets" (citing Lev). On the facts underlying investor confidence, see Bernard S. Black, "The Legal and Institutional

Preconditions for Strong Stock Markets: The Nontriviality of Securities Law," Working Paper 179 (Olin Program in Law and Economics, Stanford Law School, September 1999), who writes: "A country whose laws and related institutions foster . . . knowledge and confidence has the potential to develop a vibrant stock market that can provide capital to growing firms." See also Rafael La Porta and others, "Legal Determinants of External Finance," *Journal of Finance*, vol. 52 (1997).

107. The Nasdaq Composite Index, which is heavily weighted with technology stocks, gained 86 percent in 1999 and shot up another 22 percent in the first ten weeks of 2000, peaking at 5,055 in early March. However, it had fallen back to 3,164 in late May and closed the year at 2,470.52, a -39.3 percent change from year-end 1999. See also Floyd Norris, "The Only Sure Thing Has Been Volatility," *New York Times*, June 3, 2000, p. C1. Chan, Lakonishok, and Sougiannis, "The Stock Market Valuation of Research and Development Expenditures," report evidence that firms that are more R&D intensive have greater return volatility, once other factors are controlled for.

# Index